C000281233

# LACE

Anne Kraatz

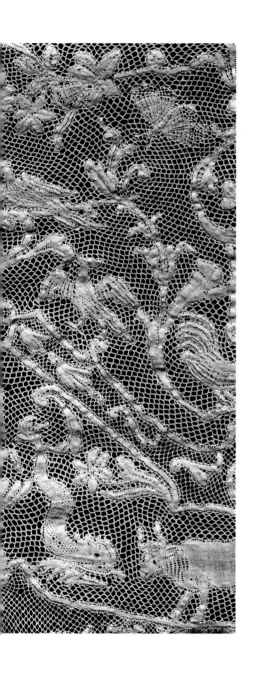

# LACE
## History and Fashion

*With 180 illustrations, 92 in colour*

Thames and Hudson

Frontispiece: Flounce (detail). Bobbins.
'Milan'. Flanders or North Italy, *c.* 1750
Linen 29 × 230 cm.
Italy, private collection

The boat surrounded by all kinds of
animals must represent Noah's Ark. There
are birds, a lion, a horse, butterflies, a bull,
and even a dolphin swimming beneath the
ship's bow

*The sizes quoted are approximate only.*
*The first figure represents the height*

Translated by PAT EARNSHAW

This edition is prepared with the
participation of the author

English translation copyright © 1989 by
Thames and Hudson Ltd, London
Originally published in France as *Dentelles*
by Éditions Adam Biro, Paris
© 1988 by Éditions Adam Biro, Paris

Printed and bound in Italy

# Contents

# Acknowledgments

Firstly I would like to give grateful thanks to Rina Brion, Cavalliere del Lavoro, who has always received me with the greatest kindness. Her collection of antique laces, begun at a time when no one thought it would have any value, was assembled with a taste so impeccable that today it contains only pieces of the highest quality. The criteria which governed Mme Brion's choice were always aesthetic. Alongside royal laces are simple peasant or naive productions representing a personal vision: quality here spells, not large production, but rather originality and perfection. Today Rina Brion's laces unquestionably form the most important private collection in Europe. This project could never have been accomplished without the personal interest which she has taken in it, and I hope I may adequately express my gratitude here.

Dr Maria Fossi Todorow, chief curator of the Palazzo Davanzati, Museo della Casa Antica Fiorentina, Florence, has as usual given me full access to the museum collection, and I thank both her and her colleagues.

Dr Kirsten Aschengreen Piacenti, chief curator of the Museo degli Argenti and the Galleria del Costume of the Palazzo Pitti, has generously allowed me to illustrate several mannequins from the Costume Gallery. I am indebted to her.

I also thank Count Girolamo Marcello, Cristina Buccellati of Gianmaria Buccellati, Milan; the Italian collectors who have preferred to remain anonymous; and Massimo Listri who has taken most of the colour photographs for this book and is himself a collector.

In France, Nadine Gasc, curator of the Textile department of the Musée des Arts Decoratifs, gave me permission to photograph some very important pieces, most of which were formerly in the collection of the Prince and Princess de la Tour d'Auvergne-Lauraguais. I am all the more grateful to her because these pieces which I myself know from having dated them at the time of their donation, have never previously been reproduced. The photographs are by Laurent Sully-James, and I thank him for his patience and cooperation.

Among French private collectors, I am especially grateful to Carmen Martinez and Viviane Grimminger of Paris; Jacqueline Daniel of Louveciennes, legal expert in toys and costume accessories to the French courts; Perle Jallot of Paris, antique dealer in Saint-Ouen; as well as to various others who did not wish to be named.

I especially thank: Yves Bottineau, Inspector-general of Museums, and Béatrix Saule, curator at the Musée National de Château de Versailles et des Trianons; Hervé Oursel, chief curator at the Musée National de la Renaissance, Château d'Ecouen;

Pierre Arizzoli-Clementel, chief curator of the Musée Historique des Tissus de Lyon, and Evelyne Gaudry, assistant curator; Patrick Le Nouëne, curator, and Mme Audiquet, assistant curator, of the Musée des Beaux-Arts et de la Dentelle de la Ville de Calais; Florence Muller, curator of l'Union Française des Arts du Costume, and Lydia Kamitsis, her assistant, for their friendly and capable help; Aude Lux, curator, Musée des Beaux-Arts de la Dentelle d'Alençon; Pierre Berge, of Yves Saint-Laurent, as well as Mme de Courrèges, for their kind cooperation; the fashion house of Jean-Louis Scherrer, and their press representative Caroline Vincent; the house of Thierry Mugler, the Gallery Gismondi, Paris; M. Coudray, of Marescot; Gisèle Haag, Giraudon; Liliane Schildge, department of Textiles of the Musée des Arts Décoratifs; Françoise Napoly of Paris; and finally, Sheila Hicks and Marie-Rose Lortet.

From other countries I would like to thank first of all Akiko Takahashi Fukai, chief curator of the Kyoto Costume Institute, who has shown much interest in this project; as well as Cees Burgers, curator of the Department of Textiles and Costumes at the Rijksmuseum, Amsterdam; Patricia Wardle; M. van Loon of the Foundation Van Loon, Amsterdam; Dr Barbara Mundt, chief curator of the Kunstgewerbemuseum in Berlin; Dr Alain Gruber, director of the Abegg Foundation in Berne; Marianne Gächter-Weber in charge of textiles at the Textilmuseum, St Gall; Marguerite Coppens, curator at the Musées Royaux d'Art et d'Histoire in Brussels; Edward Maeder, curator of the department of Textiles and Costume at the Los Angeles County Museum of Art; Marianne T. Carlano, curator of the department of Textiles and Costume at the Wadsworth Atheneum; Dilys Blum, curator of the department of Textiles and Costume at the Philadelphia Museum of Art; and finally, Maryse Volet; Doris May of Boston; Margaret Ruhland of North Gower, Ontario, Canada, and Francesca Galloway of Spink & Sons, London.

Thanks are due to Philippe Caetano who has taken most of the photographs of laces from private collections. Pascale Ogée, designer of the book, has clarified my own vision of lace by bringing to these pieces, sometimes difficult for the uninitiated to understand, a fresh and enquiring eye. In this way she has contributed much to this work.

I would like finally to pay tribute to Marie Risselin-Steenebrugen whose work laid the foundation for the revival of interest in lace, and still provides a constant source of information and inspiration.

*Paris, July 1988*

# Preface

Today the word 'lace' evokes in most minds an image of women: the skilled and diligent women who make it, and the charming and frivolous ones who wear it. The reality of lace is quite different. It was not at first particularly feminine, since men wore almost more of it than women, while its making required far more than the diligence of a lady's pastime, a pleasant pursuit to fill the hours of idleness. It required an apprenticeship which might begin at five years of age. It was punishing work which ruined the eyes and the back, and left no time for anything else. To supply the fashion-whims of men as well as women, hundreds of thousands of people worked at lace; and in the three great lace-producing countries – Italy, Belgium and France – almost the entire population was involved at one time or another.

Lace has acquired, over the centuries, a legendary evocative power. It stands for purity – what more virginal than a white wedding veil – and for eroticism – what more seductive than black lace lingerie? Charged with such associations, lace was bound at some time to return to fashion. The present-day preference for lace, so evident in the collections of couturiers and designers, suggests that that time has arrived. Yet only a few years ago the subject was of no general interest. Following numerous publications at the beginning of the century, it was no longer discussed in France or Italy except in rare articles in women's journals. Public collections were for the most part difficult of access, and historical research in this area, the systematic classification of pieces according to precise criteria, even the conditions of lace storage, were all neglected. Despite the numerous and splendid relics of this industry which have come down to us, through lack of place or means, laces were not exhibited. In Belgium the situation was somewhat different, since the collection of the Musées Royaux d'Art et d'Histoire was on permanent display, and the well-known works of E. van Overloop (1906), Lucie Paulis (1947) and Marie Risselin-Steenebrugen (1956 to 1980) show the constancy of interest in its heritage of one of the three principal centres of production.

France had nevertheless produced two fundamental works of research on the history of lace. *L'Histoire du point d'Alençon*, by Madeleine G. Despierres (1886), and *Le Poinct de France et les Centres dentelliers au XVIIᵉ et XVIIIᵉ siècle*, by Laurence de Laprade (1905), were almost the only studies to present archival documents, and they are still an essential reference source. Unfortunately these books contain few illustrations. So how do we recognize laces among the multiplicity of names, the diversity of styles and the complexity of techniques? We must continue along the paths of research opened by these authors and others and, at the same time, try to establish precise points of reference to produce a generic classification which rests as little as possible on guesswork. Above all it is essential to see, and if possible show to others, as many pieces as possible. For this, I approached in the first place the Musée des Arts Decoratifs, Paris, which has one of the most important collections of laces in Europe. Nadine Gasc, curator of the department of Textiles and Costumes, permitted me to study and work on the pieces, which I did for nearly four years; for this, I thank her. At the same time, at the Bibliothèque et Archives Nationales, I studied the documents concerning this industry. I was fascinated among other things by the 'lace war' between the France of Louis XIV and Colbert and the Republic of Venice, which was a serious business at that time (see chapter 2). I was able to make two long visits to Italy thanks to two grants awarded me by the Gladys Krieble Delmas Foundation of New York, to research in the Venetian archives. I was able to report on the wealth of documents about lace in the Archivio di Stato. In particular I discovered the inventory of a Venetian merchant, dated 1671, which contained a wealth of information about the lace trade at that time. In 1981 the chief curator of the Palazzo Davanzati,

Museo della Casa Fiorentina Antica, Dr Maria Fossi Todorow, asked me to help her to select pieces and write the entries for a catalogue for an exhibition of laces to be organized that year at the palace by Marina Carmignani. This exhibition was one of the first of its kind in Italy, after that of the Musée Poldi-Pezzoli in Milan, put on in 1977 by the museum's director, Alessandra Mottola-Molfino. The importance of the Davanzati collection is that it is the only collection in a state museum which is permanently open to the public. The quality, if not the quantity of the pieces, and the method used to display and conserve them, are remarkable.

In Venice, the lace school of Burano has been revived, and a museum has been set up in the school where numerous exhibitions of antique and modern laces are held. For some time now the other lace regions of Italy – Genoa, Fruili, Abruzzi – have been showing an interest in their lace-making heritage and organizing exhibitions, conferences and workshops.

In France, no major exhibitions on this theme had been held since the celebrated exhibition at the Palais Galliéra in 1904. Some eighty years later, in 1983, I suggested to Mlle Delpierre, then chief curator of the Musée de la Mode et du Costume de la Ville de Paris, that the time was ripe for another. She agreed with enthusiasm, and we set to work. The result was an exhibition of three hundred pieces of lace from public and private collections, both French and others, and in addition one hundred costumes from the museum's collection.

In the course of my research for this exhibition I was able to study laces of great beauty in the reserve collections of a number of museums. Two collections in particular were of great interest. That of the Musée National de la Renaissance (formerly the collection of the Musée de Cluny) contained important pieces which Alain Erlande-Brandenburg, at that time chief curator of the museum, willingly lent for the Palais Galliéra exhibition. As for that of the Musée Historique des Tissus de Lyon, I

organized an exhibition of one hundred of their pieces in September 1983, at the request of the assistant curator, Evelyne Gaudry.

All these exhibitions responded to three needs. In the first place they allowed a showing to the public of what had long been hidden, namely the widest possible choice of laces reflecting the diversity of techniques and designs of all periods. They also allowed the clearing up of misunderstandings, even the correction of errors, concerning places of production, and dating of laces. Although the almost total absence of documented pieces, the amplitude of the production over the centuries, and the international nature of the lace trade, make a precise classification of individual pieces difficult, nevertheless the analysis of technique and style, with comparisons between lace and the productions of the other decorative arts, allows us in most instances to place the pieces within a relatively precise chronological and aesthetic framework. Finally, they indicated the importance of lace in the artistic and economic life of the principal producing countries, and in fashion.

For the drafting of the present work I decided to adopt the approach I had used for the exhibitions, while using chiefly previously unpublished illustrations. My conversations with the public during these exhibitions had convinced me that they wanted precise information about lace rather than anecdotes: to learn the technical and design characteristics of each, to be able to place the great laces in their social and historical contexts, and to distinguish antique laces from copies. I have attempted, therefore, within the limits of the present work, to provide at least the beginnings of a response to these requests. However, 'the study of lace is complex and delicate. Few sciences present less of absolute truth'. This observation by L. Deshairs, in 1906 in the revue *Art et Décoration*, is no less true today.

A. K.

Furnishing flounce (detail). Needle. 'Point de France'. France, Royal manufactory, perhaps Sedan, 1685–1715 Linen 61 × 305 cm Ecouen, Musée National de la Renaissance; inv. E. Cl. 14285 Formerly collection of the Musée de Cluny, gift of Baron Philippe de Rothschild

The inspiration of this design is certainly Indo-Persian, even if the twisted columns flanking the central pineapple or pine-cone motif recall those of the *baldacchino* in St Peter's, Rome, by Bernini. The inwardly curving elements – leafy, veined and fretted – are treated with a richness of decorative stitches of unparalleled virtuosity. The whole produces a kaleidoscopic effect, as if variegated threads had been used instead of white only. The author's researches on this piece are forthcoming

Dressing-table cover (detail)
Needle. 'Reticella' and 'punto in aria'
Italy, *c.* 1600.
Linen 103 × 130 cm
Florence, Palazzo Davanzati; inv. Stoffe, 1339, gift of Giorgio Calligaris; cat. no. 9

The bands of linen are decorated with motifs in reticella and bordered by other
motifs in punto in aria. Pieces of this kind are typical of the productions of the first
years of the sixteenth century. Many copies were made in the nineteenth century.
The donor of this piece, Giorgio Calligaris, was until recently an important lace
merchant-manufacturer

# THE SIXTEENTH CENTURY

# OPENWORK

*Woman at her toilet*
French school of the seventeenth century, *c.* 1600. Oil on canvas
Montauban, Musée Ingres

The young woman's hair falls over her peignoir of fine batiste decorated with
insertions and edgings of needle-made reticella and punto in aria. The cloth which
covers the table is made up of squares of embroidered linen alternating with squares
of reticella

Needle lace is undoubtedly the invention of Venetian embroiderers who in the 1540s had a brilliant idea: that of reversing the technique of drawn threadwork. This process consisted in removing from a length of woven cloth a certain number of weft threads and covering the remaining warps and wefts with buttonhole stitches, so as to form a strongly held grid, then casting further threads between the elements of the supporting grid and covering them with buttonhole stitches also. The technique of openwork embroidery is still practised today.

When towards the beginning of the sixteenth century the desire for openness became greater, more and more threads had to be removed to achieve the required effect. This was tedious and also somewhat illogical: a lot of time was simply wasted in undoing the work of the weaver. Approaching the task from the opposite direction, the Venetian embroiderers decided to build for themselves the necessary foundation of threads. Thus needle lace was born. Unlike embroidery, the work was no longer done on a separate supporting fabric, but instead all the components grew together as the work progressed. The technique of drawnwork with its skeleton of woven fabric is called *reticella*, an Italian word meaning a grid or network. When the foundation is constructed by the lacemakers over a temporary support, it is called *punto in aria* – literally, 'stitches in the air'. The two products are sometimes difficult to distinguish with the naked eye.

Bobbin lace, on the other hand, is certainly derived from a weaving of braids technique, that of 'passementerie'. The craft was practised originally by members of the corporation of passementiers who wove ribbons, galoons and other edgings on a loom, or plaited them on long cushions using pins to hold the criss-crossed threads in place. To prevent the threads becoming tangled they were wound on weights made of lead, bone or wood, and these weights or rudimentary spools eventually became the wooden bobbins of the lacemakers.

The exact time and place of the transition from one technique to the other is not known, but it is generally agreed that it happened simultaneously in Flanders (probably in the region of Antwerp) and in Italy (almost certainly in Venice) at the end of the first quarter of the sixteenth century. It is scarcely surprising that we have no more precise information on the date and place of this transformation, for the invention of a technique never comes to full fruition immediately. Even after the idea of lace as an autonomous structure had been universally understood, embroiderers undoubtedly continued to draw threads and embroider, and passementiers to weave passements on a loom. The new techniques certainly did not supplant the old completely for several decades after their invention.

That regions so far apart as northern Italy and Flanders arrived at the invention of lace at the same period is just one of the manifestations of the universality of taste characteristic of the Renaissance. What was fashionable one day in Venice, in the middle of the sixteenth century, would almost immediately become fashionable in Antwerp, Paris or London. The ideal vehicles for this rapid diffusion, which no boundaries or frontiers could stop, were the pattern books. It is not by chance that the universal adoption of lace coincided with the great extension of printing, of which Venice and Antwerp were two of the most important centres at that time.

The first pattern book, still relevant to embroidery but already presenting an increased amount of openwork, was that of Mathio Pagano, entitled *Giardinetto novo di punti tagliati et gropposi per exercito e ornamento delle donne* ('A new collection of cutwork and embroidery for the practise and ornamentation of ladies'). This book was published in Venice in 1542 and was immediately reprinted, sometimes with local additions, by European publishers from Antwerp to Paris by way of Augsburg and Nüremberg. In all, it was reprinted some thirty times. *Le Pompe* (1557), an

Bed-cover. Needle, embroidered filet. Dated 1588
Linen 105 × 105 cm
Paris, Musée des Arts Décoratifs; inv. 52842. Formerly collection of the Prince and Princess de la Tour d'Auvergne-Lauraguais

The bed-cover carries the date 1588 and the inscription *Vertu pas tout* (Virtue is not everything), with the signature 'Alis de Baillœul'. This phrase, as well as the presence of the siren combing her long hair in front of a mirror, indicate that the author was a courtesan. The siren symbolizes lust and the mirror vanity

*And there we were unwrapping them slowly and looking at the designs which unrolled before our eyes. . . . First came bands of Italian work, tough pieces with drawn threads in which everything was repeated over and over. . . . Then all at once a whole succession of our glances would be barred with Venetian needlepoint, as though we had been cloisters or prisons. Mama sighed . . . 'One knows so little about all that' . . .*

RAINER MARIA RILKE
*The Notebooks of Malte Laurids-Brigge*

anonymous work, again published in Venice, was the first book to include patterns for bobbin laces. It is an important work because it indicates to readers the exact number of bobbins necessary for the working of certain patterns.

Technical instructions were rarely included in these pattern books, which until the end of the century were directed mostly to ladies of the nobility, or at least 'to women of good morals', of whom it could be taken for granted that they knew how to ply a needle. Sewing, embroidery, even weaving, were among the activities to which all honest women were expected to devote themselves from earliest childhood. This was true for all classes of society, for whom these activities were thought to constitute a sort of moral guarantee against idleness. Examples of well-born needlewomen are not lacking at this period. There was Mary Queen of Scots, who certainly had leisure for embroidery during her long captivity, and Catherine de Médicis (queen of Henri II of France). It is to the second that the most celebrated of all lace pattern books is dedicated, that of the Venetian Vinciolo, who had settled in France at the invitation of Catherine herself, according to some authorities. *Les singuliers et nouveaux pourtraicts du seigneur Federic de Vinciolo Venitien, pour touttes sortes d'ouvrages de Lingerie* ('Unusual and New

Flounce (detail). Needle, framed with bobbin strands. 'Punto in aria'. Italy, probably Venice, *c.* 1600
Linen 14 × 240 cm
Italy, private collection

This flounce, of excellent workmanship, was doubtless intended to border a ruff or a raised collar. The design of alternating rosettes is faithfully copied from a pattern by Vinciolo

Designs, by Signor Federico di Vinciolo, Venetian, for all sorts of Needlework'), published in Paris in 1587, set out patterns for cutwork – in fact true needle laces – and for embroidered filet.

Filet is not properly speaking a lace. It consists of an embroidery in linen or darning stitch on a network of square, knotted meshes, made beforehand using a shuttle and a frame. Although knotted filet is known from antiquity, no one apparently had the idea of embroidering it before the beginning of the sixteenth century. Its appearance then was another expression of the new taste for openwork and lightness. Embroidered filet played a very important role in interior decoration right through the sixteenth century and during part of the seventeenth. In addition, it was much used in conjunction with needle lace, especially for large furnishing pieces such as counterpanes or bed-valances. It is said that Catherine de Médicis herself loved to make filet, and the

Bracelets (face and reverse sides), Mario Bucellati, 1929 and 1930
White and yellow pierced gold, diamonds and rose-cut diamonds 5 × 20 cm
Milan, collection Gianmaria Bucellati

These bracelets of precious-metal lace are obviously inspired by late sixteenth-century reticella, from which the arrangement of squares enclosing rosettes, here in diamonds, has been borrowed. Equally they are copying seventeenth-century Venetian laces by imitating the ground of brides linking the geometric elements. Lace for a long time was a status symbol as important and often as costly as jewels. This goldsmith's work, entirely hand-made, is a most successful transposition, both aesthetically and symbolically, of the preciousness inherent in lace

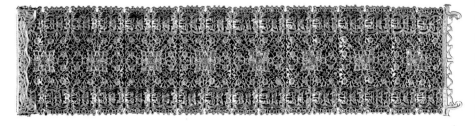

inventory of her goods at her death listed a large number of pieces, including several complete bed-furnishings and almost a thousand squares with motifs of 'geometric and floral patterns'. Filet therefore has its place within the present work because it is universally regarded as a lace, especially when made of white thread, as is usually the case. However, there was nothing to prevent the use of coloured threads, and several examples of polychrome embroideries on filet survive from this period. Embroidered filet disappeared from inventories about the middle of the seventeenth century. This does not mean that it was no longer made, since pattern books for embroidered filet continued to be published, most notably in Germany, up to the 1750s, but by then it no longer had any market value and was considered a mere pastime for ladies.

From 1587 to 1658, some forty editions of Vinciolo's book would be published with few modifications. The book of another Venetian, Cesare Vecellio, said to be related to Titian, was to become equally celebrated. This was *La Corona delle nobili et virtuose donne*, which appeared in Venice in 1593. In it, the author presents patterns for 'stitches in the air, cutwork and reticella', and states that many of them could be worked equally well with bobbins.

The numerous pattern books published in Germany indicate the importance of lace-making there at that period. The book of Johann Siebmacher, for example, published in Nüremberg in 1597, and that of Bernhart Jobin, published in Strasburg in 1583, were to enjoy an immense and lasting success, equal to that of their Italian contemporaries.

These four books were to be among the most widely used when, during the nineteenth century, the fashion for the Renaissance style gave rise to a veritable copy industry, in lace as in the other applied arts. I shall return to the importance of copies and adaptations of antique laces in the chapter devoted to the nineteenth century.

The list of pattern books is long. It is notable that it includes only two by celebrated women

Page of a lace pattern book (details). Anonymous, 1623 Paris, Bibliothèque Nationale

Patterns for 'bobbin passements'. These patterns were very original for the period, and they do not appear to have enjoyed as great a success as others which were more conventional and doubtless easier to make

authors: those of Isabeta Catanea Parasole and Lucretia Romana, whose pattern books for bobbin and needle laces appeared in 1600 in Rome and in 1620 in Venice respectively.

What kind of patterns did these books offer? Mostly geometric motifs – stars, rosettes, mosaics of triangles, squares or lozenges – but also more naturalistic forms – animals, people, flowers and scrolls, which were, however, always enclosed within a geometric frame. The new techniques no longer required such a rigid shape, but it took the lacemakers a certain time to perceive and fully exploit their inherent possibilities.

This severe aesthetic approach is curiously at variance with what was happening in the other areas of decorative art – woven fabrics, embroideries, inlaid work in wood or marble, bookbinding etc. There, the style of ornaments called 'grotesques' predominated. It consists of floral elements, rosettes, foliated scrolls, in the middle of which frolicked cupids and fantastic animals. Such whimsical imagery was often

used in the decoration of embroidered filets (as opposed to real lace) where mythological figures, biblical scenes and allegories abound. It must be said that the technique of embroidered filet is more quickly mastered than that of lace, and that numerous patterns for cross-stitch embroidery, for example, can easily be transposed for filet work.

There is little stylistic correspondence, therefore, between the lace patterns of the years 1540 to 1615 and other productions of that period. Doubtless the impersonality of the motifs contributed to the enormous success lace enjoyed across the whole of Europe: for what were more likely to break the seal of an outdated provincialism than geometrical elements whose linear precision is universally understood, and which were, moreover, easily arranged in an infinite variety of combinations by the least experienced of women. Both bobbin and needle laces were geometrical, the preferred form of the first being the downward-pointing triangle like a tooth (*dent*) – from which comes the French word for lace (*dentelle*) – and that of the second, a square.

For as long as the aspect of laces remained geometrical, it is in my view very difficult to determine their date and place of production. When motifs and techniques are exactly similar it would seem pointless to attempt to attribute this or that piece of needle or bobbin lace to this or that precise region. Archival documents show fairly conclusively that lace-production had already extended throughout the whole of Europe from the third quarter of the sixteenth century, or even earlier.

If pattern books were directed to well-bred ladies, in reality they probably had the professionals in mind as well. As far as needle lace was concerned, these professionals were also women, doubtless for the most part seamstresses working for the corporation of linen-drapers, as well as nuns, and the inmates of hospitals or other charitable institutions. The trade in needle lace was probably fairly limited

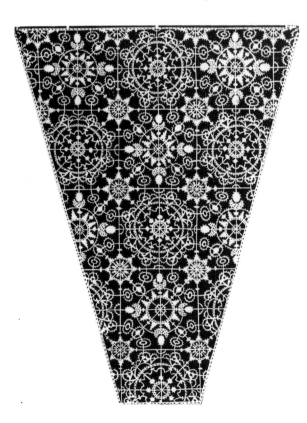

M. La.     Connestable. desdiguires

then. For bobbin laces, it seems the situation was different, for the corporations of passement-makers were immediately interested in the new technique, and attempted to acquire the monopoly of its manufacture. Unlike the passementerie looms, however, the equipment for the manufacture of bobbin lace – a cushion filled with straw and a few bobbins of turned wood – could easily be made and transported by anyone. It was therefore not possible to submit the ownership of its tools to the rigid rules of a corporation. The passementiers, faced with the competition of what one would nowadays call independent operatives, were forced to give up the making of bobbin lace. In addition, the members, all male, of the corporation of passementiers, as of that of embroiderers, disdained working with thread – that is, white linen – because one of their most important privileges was that of embroidering or weaving threads of precious metal. That the craft of lacemaking was almost entirely confined to women doubtless explains why those who practised it never

formed their own corporation, despite the economic importance of their production, which in certain places and periods was at least as great as that of weaving or embroidery.

## FASHION

When, around 1580, ruffs edged with lace became fashionable, the great lengths of fabric needed for the purpose could scarcely be supplied any longer by home-handicrafts. Lace became a merchandise sold by the yard by haberdashers, who obtained it then from the more or less family-based workshops which had sprung up spontaneously in the towns and villages, and from convents and orphanages where labour was cheap and plentiful. These two different sources of production coexisted without difficulty, despite the lack of central organization, for there were no problems of outlet. Demand was strong and constant because fashion demanded an ever-increasing display of lace. Even if all the great cities were not as rich at the end of the sixteenth century as Venice (in reality that city was already in decline and living largely beyond its means) or Antwerp (in full prosperity), neither the nobility nor the rising European merchant class – from the British Isles to Bohemia and from Sweden to Portugal, not forgetting Paris – could imagine elegance without lace.

The essential feature of the fashion of the years 1560 to 1620 was the large lace ruff or raised collar. Although the size and the shape of this accessory might vary a little between regions, it was always made with similar laces. Only in Venice was the round Spanish ruff rarely worn. Venetian women always preferred a large fan-shaped collar, held up straight above the shoulders by a metal frame, which displayed the geometric motifs of the needle lace to better advantage than could the multiple pleating of ruffs. In Florence, on the other hand, the great round ruff completely encircling the neck was adopted with enthusiasm at first, later evolving

LVCREZIA RICA          SOLI · NE ZANCHINI ·

*Henri II de Montmorency*, French school of the seventeenth century, 1625–30
Oil on canvas
Paris, Musée Carnavalet

The figure wears a collar raised on either side of the face by a metal support (underpropper) which holds it in position. The collar is made of linen decorated with wide insertions and edging of punto in aria

into a half-ruff open in front, sometimes of truly gigantic proportions. In Flanders the formal portraits of the time, of which numerous examples have survived, show very clearly that the ruff or lace collar was regarded as an indispensable accessory. Flemish women of the end of the sixteenth century nearly always wore a closed ruff with three or even four rows of bobbin lace, while their bonnets were of needle lace, often embroidered with pearls. In England extravagance reigned, and the ruffs of Queen Elizabeth I are famous. Englishmen, like Frenchmen, preferred the large square collar of needle lace, mounted on an underpropper in the shape of a tray, against which the single earring they favoured could be exhibited. All these collars were worn, naturally, with matching cuffs, sashes and handkerchiefs. As for Frenchwomen, they used lace with a restraint in keeping with their taste for a rather austere elegance. In France, it was not so much a question of putting lace everywhere as of placing it where it most flattered the wearer.

Enormous quantities of white linen lace were now needed to trim all these ruffs, while clothing and furnishings were also trimmed with a profusion of laces, although more often than not these were of polychrome silk or gold thread, rather than white linen. Inventories of the time preserve numerous records of such costly laces, but unfortunately few of the laces themselves have survived. Silk stands up to the passage of time much less well than linen. As for gold and silver laces, even fewer are left, because most of them were melted down to recover the precious metal of which they were made.

It seems that Spain produced a quantity of gold and silver laces at the time when she still possessed the greatest reserves of these metals in Europe, that is, up to the end of the sixteenth century. Indeed, the name 'point d'Espagne' was used for metal laces up to the mid-seventeenth century, although the most extensive production was by then elsewhere, especially in France and Italy.

Laces, be they of linen, polychrome silks or gold and silver, were expensive, and the authorities of the various states viewed their subjects' expenditure on luxurious and frivolous attire with disapproval, all the more so because many of these laces were imported – except possibly in Italy, where production was intensive enough to satisfy both local consump-

*Portrait of a Woman*,
Gheeraerts, dated 1619
Oil on canvas
London, Roy Miles Fine
Paintings

The young woman wears a
single-layered ruff, fastened
very high under the chin, a
shawl collar and long cuffs
of bobbin lace worked in
gold thread, as well as
bands of needle-made
reticella in the slits of the
sleeves of her gown. The
geometric motifs of these
laces contrasts strikingly
with the very naturalistic
flowers in the cut velvet of
which her gown is made

Page 20
Man's collar. Needle within
bobbin-made frames.
'Reticella' and 'punto in
aria'. Italy or France,
1600–20
Linen 18 × 96 cm
Italy, private collection

This large collar was
intended to be supported
by a metal underpropper
and to be worn raised up.
Like all the pieces of this
period, it was not made as
a whole, but as a number
of bands cut and then
joined to make the shape.
Very few intact examples of
this type of collar have
survived because of the
practice of re-using the
laces when the original
shape was no longer
fashionable

tion and export. It has often been written that the sumptuary laws were promulgated to stem the outflow of currency from one state to another. This was only partially the reason. The edicts or ordinances against the wearing of laces, pronounced by all the European states since laces first appeared, laid as much stress, if not more, on two other considerations. The display of luxury was condemned not only for economic reasons – a false argument, since the manufacture of lace gave work to many people – but also for social and moral reasons. Pride was a sin often publicly condemned by the Catholic Church, though herself a great consumer of lace of all kinds, and severely disapproved of by the Protestant Church, which made austerity in everything its keynote. In addition, the riches displayed gave rise to envy in persons of modest means who could not acquire them for themselves. The unhealthy social climate that resulted was dangerous in the longer or shorter term to the stability of states, and herein, precisely, lay the social purpose of these laws: for how does one distinguish an aristocrat from a merchant, a merchant from a rich farmer, a virtuous middle-class wife from a girl of doubtful morals, if everyone wears the same lace? The King of France, Henri III, in a public pronouncement in July 1576, wondered '. . . that the simple gentlemen show themselves every day as superbly adorned as if they were dukes or barons, and . . . there are at present no distinctions between the commoners and the nobles, whether in themselves or in their wives . . .'. The hierarchy of the classes is not, as is generally supposed, an immovable feature of monarchical regimes; in order to preserve it, it is necessary to exercise a degree of vigilance.

The sumptuary laws set out, therefore, to forbid the wearing of lace to nearly all the social classes except the highest – the royal family and nobles above a certain rank – or at least, to dictate its size and position on clothes in the minutest detail. In Venice, for example, the population of the Jewish ghetto whose dress was regulated by special sumptuary laws, could not wear any white needle lace nor any gold or silver lace. White thread bobbin laces were allowed, but they must not exceed four fingers' breadth; for the women's head veils, only black bobbin lace, not needle, was permitted. In France and elsewhere, the authorities attempted to introduce a total prohibition on the manufacture of gold and silver laces, since the precious metals were reserved primarily for the minting of coins. In fact, they succeeded in increasing fraud, for tinsel was substituted in the majority of cases for pure gold but the prices remained the same. In order to make an example, laces were periodically seized and burned in the main square, to little avail.

These sumptuary laws, so pompously specific in their prescriptions, provide an accurate commentary on the importance of lace in setting both aesthetic and social standards. More than jewels or rich fabrics, lace was truly a status symbol *par excellence* at the end of the sixteenth century, and remained, throughout the constant evolutions of fashion, far more than a simple piece of frippery. Lace might sometimes be unfashionable; it could never be out of favour. Its very name suffices to evoke a vision of luxury and elegance indissolubly linked to the notion of class.

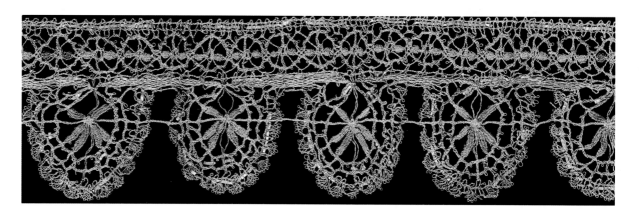

# The great laces of the Renaissance and their characteristics

Frontispiece of the pattern book of Gasparo Crivellari. Italy, 1580–1610. German facsimile, nineteenth century Paris, Bibliothèque des Arts Décoratifs; collection Maciet

The designs of this little-known pattern book are very similar to those in the collar with underpropper worn by Henri II de Montmorency (see p. 20)

Page 25
Man's collar. 'Reticella' and 'punto in aria'. Europe, perhaps Italy, c. 1610
Linen depth 35 cm
Amsterdam, Rijksmuseum; inv. N.B. 14162

The designs of this celebrated collar are similar to the patterns in the book by Gasparo Crivellari. A little interlaced bobbin border finishes the sides of the collar on a level with the shoulders. The tassels which serve to tie the collar beneath the chin are in punto in aria, probably worked over a stiff metal thread

*The needle laces of this period are most often designated by their Italian names which are therefore given first below.*

## NEEDLE LACES

### Punto tagliato (Cutwork)

Cutwork is not a lace. It is worked on a pre-made and permanent support, a woven cloth. This is cut wherever openings are required, and the edges of the openings thus made are strengthened with overcasting or buttonhole stitches. As the number and size of the holes increases, so the work approaches the following stage, that of reticella. The idea, bold in its conception, of creating empty spots in a fabric, appeared towards the beginning of the sixteenth century. It was the first and indispensable aesthetic step towards the development of lace.

### Reticella

This is the ancestor of all needle laces, but its technique still requires a pre-existing support. Most of the threads are drawn out from a band of cloth, leaving only a few vertical and a few horizontal strands which are then strengthened with buttonhole stitching. They are needed to serve as a support for other threads which are cast across the spaces thus created and also covered with buttonhole stitches. The frame of the motifs so formed is necessarily geometric because it is made by the threads of the cloth which intersect at right angles. Reticella can be distinguished from the geometric form of punto in aria, which followed, by the residue of woven cloth discernible beneath the points of joining at the top and bottom.

Instead of unpicking the woven fabric, which is tedious and illogical, the necessary framework of threads is constructed on a temporary support which is removed once the work is finished. This is the technical starting-point for the concept of lace. At first, the motifs remained geometric because the forms of expression which the new method made possible were not yet understood. The horizontal sides were not always made of threads couched to a temporary support, and strengthened. Frequently they were made by means of braids worked by bobbins, or of threads plaited by hand, which further increased the speed of production. The stitches were usually worked in white linen thread, sometimes mingled with threads of gold or silver, but almost never mixed with coloured threads. Since very little linen was dyed, in order to make coloured lace it would have been necessary to use coloured silks, of which the tension and twist were different from those of linen, so that the two were difficult to work together.

The above three techniques are often referred to under the generic name 'Venice', whatever the date and place of their production.

## BOBBIN LACES

### Passements

This is a general term applied to all the bobbin laces of the sixteenth and seventeenth centuries, whether made of white linen, coloured silks or gold or silver thread. They are continuous-thread (*à fils continus*) laces, the borders of which are nearly always in the

form of scallops, at first more or less pointed, later rounded. The motifs are fairly similar to those of needle laces – rosettes, grids, triangles – but they are much lighter in aspect. Bobbin-made passements, particularly those from Flanders, were used to edge ruffs in preference to needle laces precisely because of this lightness.

## FILET

Filet is not a lace, since in it the motifs are embroidered on a pre-existing and permanent support, the filet itself. The technique of filet is a system of square

Panel (detail). Needle, framed with bobbin strands. 'Reticella' and 'punto in aria'. Europe, perhaps southern Italy, 1620–25
Linen 106 × 180 cm
St Gall, Textilmuseum; inv. LT 696

The tight doublet and long breeches tucked into the boots of the male figure enable us to place the lace in the 1620s. The naive design of this piece contrasts with its perfect workmanship

Page 26
Furnishing drape (detail). Needle. Embroidered filet. France or Italy, *c.* 1580
Linen and polychrome silk, 130 × 180 cm
Private collection

The decoration of this piece is adapted from the 'grotesques' in the loges of the Vatican, painted by the pupils of Raphael about 1520, which provided a fertile source of inspiration for embroideries and tapestries up to the end of the seventeenth century

meshes, knotted at the corners, and made with a shuttle or a needle. It is much earlier than lace, having been known from antiquity.

However, no one appears to have conceived the idea of embroidering filet before the beginning of the sixteenth century – that is, a little before the appearance of the new techniques which were to give rise to lace. Embroidered filet is not to be confused with *buratto*, a sort of openwork canvas (gauze) woven on a loom, and most often made of hemp dyed black. It was used for embroidery in the same way as filet, but nearly always embroidered with multicoloured silk threads.

Below and page 29
Bed-cover details. Needle.
Embroidered filet, cutwork,
'reticella' and 'punto in
aria'. France or Flanders,
1580–1620
Linen 180 × 130 cm
Paris, Musée des Arts
Décoratifs

The contrast between the squares of reticella with their mosaic effect, and the squares of embroidered filet showing allegorical or anecdotal scenes, is here particularly happy. The outer border of embroidered filet is like a magic lantern show with huntsmen, angels, turretted castles, a noble lady in a cart drawn by geese, and another riding an elephant – a detail which suggests that it could be a Flemish work, in the spirit of the carnival processions or fairs where all sorts of animals took part. This bed-cover has been copied many times. In the 1900s the firm of Melville and Zieffer offered copies completely finished, or for people to mount themselves. Below: detail

Pillow-case. Needle. Cutwork, 'reticella', 'punto in aria' and surface embroidery. Italy, *c.* 1600
Linen 58 × 42 cm
Florence, Palazzo Davanzati; inv. Stoffe 1375; cat. no. 7

Pillows of coloured silk were slipped inside these covers so that the lace motifs were perfectly displayed. Italian inventories of this period include a number of such pillow-cases made for show, and they frequently appear in the paintings of Venetian and Flemish masters, and also in tapestries

Handkerchief (detail). Needle. 'Venetian point plat'. Italy, *c.* 1645
Linen 96 × 42 cm
Italy, private collection

The handkerchief border is completely free of all geometric restraint, so that it can no longer be called punto in aria. Lace of this kind must be described under the generic term 'Venetian point plat'. There is no raised work, but the solid areas show the first appearance of decorative stitches. Note the central motif of the Indian with plumed head-dress

*Young Dutchwoman* (detail),
Thomas de Keyser, *c.* 1630
Tarbes, Musée Massey

The pleated cuff is
bordered with bobbin-made
passements with a design of
stylized tulips

Page 33
Bed-cover (detail). Needle.
'Reticella' and 'punto in
aria'. France, 1595–1615
Linen 180 × 130 cm
Paris, Musée des Arts
Décoratifs; inv. 110 (dépot
du Louvre)

This is one of the most
important pieces of lace
preserved in France. Its
rich design includes people
and animals of all kinds.
The detail illustrated shows
two young people on either
side of the fountain of
youth. The young man is
dressed in Spanish style
with padded trunk hose.
The young woman wears a
farthingale with a very
small waist. Her coif forms
two wings on either side,
coming to a point at the
front, in the style made
fashionable by Catherine de
Médicis in the 1560s,
during her widowhood. A
mermaid looks in a mirror
on the right

Stomacher. Needle and
bobbin. 'Reticella', 'punto
in aria' and 'passements'.
Italy (?), *c.* 1620
Linen 35 × 50 cm
Florence, Palazzo
Davanzati; inv. Bargello
4348; cat. no. 10

The shape of stomachers
scarcely varied between the
1550s and the 1770s. Here
the main part is made by
the joining together of
pieces of reticella with a
very stylized design of
animals, indicating a
peasant or provincial
production. The border on
the other hand is bobbin-
made, with rosettes in the
classic style of passements
of the period. The
mounting as a stomacher is
later

Flounce (detail).
Needle. 'Venetian gros point'. Venice, *c.* 1670
Linen 55 × 100 cm
Florence, Palazzo Davanzati; inv. Bargello Varie 92; cat. no. 21

A typical example of the type of lace in which the sculptural
effect is ideally suited to masculine clothes

# THE SEVENTEENTH CENTURY

# MASCULINITY

*Portrait of a member of the Chigi family*,
Jacob Ferdinand Voet
Oil on canvas, *c.* 1670
Alençon, Musée des Beaux-Arts et de la Dentelle

The young Italian aristocrat wears a rabat of Venetian
gros point with matching cuffs. His coat is trimmed with
black bobbin lace

In the seventeenth century lace passed through three successive phases: the first during the years 1620 to 1650, when a movement towards a diversification of styles and methods appeared; the second, from 1650 to around 1670, when Venetian gros point ruled the world unchallenged; and the third, from 1670 to 1690, when the development of point de France assured French domination of the market.

At the beginning of the century, the intellectual and aesthetic frontiers opened by the Renaissance were closed again. A new nationalism appeared, accentuated by the now irreversible division between Catholic and Protestant Europe. At an economic level, this was a time of competition. Each country manufactured for itself, and even exported, the products necessary for elegance, rather than importing them at great expense. This led to commercial conflict, of which the rivalry between Venice and the France of Louis XIV was the harshest manifestation, and then to the use of secret agents, coded letters and manipulation of the workers. We shall return to these developments.

Towards 1620 the long reign of the ruff ended. It was replaced by large flat collars, turned down over the shoulders, which were worn by both men and women. The pointed teeth of the passements, the reticellas with their crystalline geometry, light and stiff in appearance, gave place to heavier and more opaque laces. The emphasis on empty space essential in the preceding century was no longer indispensable.

The emerging designs with their freer forms, their broader features, their naturalistic elements, could not have been rendered except with an increase in size of the solid areas. This change of style was heralded by the pattern book of Wilhelm Hoffman, published in Frankfurt in 1604, and confirmed by that of Bartolomeo Danieli, the first edition of which appeared in Bologna in 1610. The patterns of Danieli are characterized by the use of wreaths and curves, arranged in an architectural manner around a central motif, often a stylized vase of flowers. The compositions were arranged heightwise of the lace, so that for the first time lace had a direction, in contrast to the geometric motifs of the previous century which could be read equally well from bottom to top or from right to left.

Danieli's book was a great success, and although it was reprinted with new patterns up

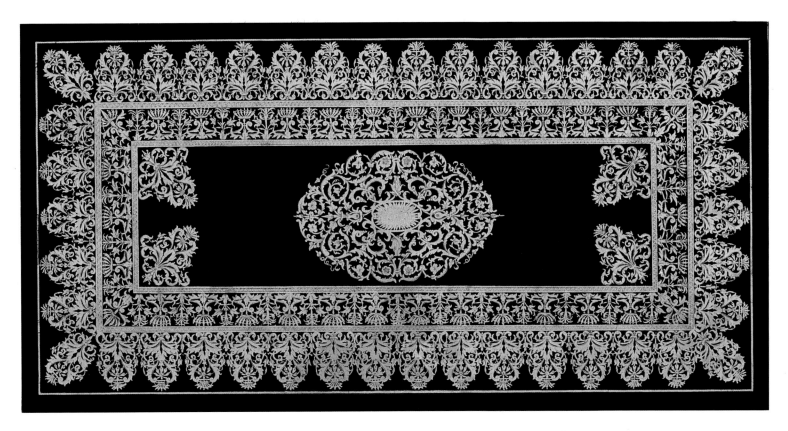

to 1648, they continued in the same vein, not surprisingly, since it accurately reflected the aesthetic preoccupations of the time. The carnations, narcissi and tulips which abounded there were the flowers which Europeans had discovered thanks to the Dutch commerce with the Indies. Contrary to the situation in the preceding century, Danieli's patterns were used for the other applied arts as well as for lace. They appeared in marble, in marquetries of wood or stone, in the decoration of bookbindings, in ironwork and embroidery. It was thus appropriate that his book was dedicated not only to the usual 'virtuous and skilful wives and maidens', but also to draughtsmen, sculptors, embroiderers and cabinetmakers. However, it was to be the last book of its type, for the manufacture of lace no longer proceeded at the level of a ladies' pastime, but had become a vast commercial enterprise.

In the first half of the seventeenth century the towns of Flanders were among the most prosperous in Europe. The Dutch, ahead of all the world, had established their East India Company in 1602. Since then, they had not ceased to extend their commercial domination of the East, where they supplanted Venice. The activity which resulted from this, in the great ports such as Amsterdam and Antwerp, had important economic repercussions over that whole region and beyond. Thus conditions for a general increase in the production of consumer goods were created. The age was favourable to the expansion of the lace industry in a geographical area where the raw material was abundant and where, too, bleaching and spinning were understood in an incomparable manner. The towns of Mechlin, Binche, Bruges and Brussels dedicated themselves to lace, and worked out little by little the style and the techniques to which their names remain attached, and which have made them famous. However this evolution was rather slow – it did not truly come to fruition until the end of the

Table. Scagliola (marquetry of bone powder on black marble). *c.* 1640
65.5 × 131 cm
Paris, Galerie Gismondi

The decoration of the table is inspired by, if not actually copied from, the lace designs of Danieli. Similar decorations on a smaller scale would be just as likely to occur on bookbindings of the period

Page 36
Page of a pattern book, Bartolomeo Danieli. Bologna, *c.* 1639
Paris, Bibliothèque des Arts Décoratifs; coll. Maciet

Originally intended for lace, these patterns were extremely popular in all areas of decorative art at that time

century – and meanwhile the whole of Flanders made more or less the same bobbin lace.

As for France, all the north, where the cultivation of flax was also very widespread, applied itself to lacemaking, from Calais and Lille in the west to Sedan in the east, and including Arras a little further south. Normandy too was occupied with lace work, both needle and bobbin, and there are contemporary references to laces or passements from Le Havre, Dieppe, Rouen and Honfleur. The region of the Oise, to the north of Paris, was particularly devoted to the production of silk laces, often black, and of metal laces. Lyons also produced gold and silver laces, although these were more often than not made of tinsel.

During this time Italy lived on its reputation and was not at first very good at adapting itself to modern trends. Its lace-production was extensive, but it lacked artistic and commercial dynamism. The documents of the time show that the quantities of Flemish lace imported into Italy, and particularly to Venice, were very considerable. The laces of Genoa ended by being replaced with those from Flanders. Venice, occupied with her war against Austria, reacted by producing a kind of lace known as 'flat Venetian' (Venetian point plat). Although the solid areas were worked entirely with the needle, its characteristic form was a uniform tape linked by picoted brides. Thus in the 1640s, flat Venetian was seeking to imitate bobbin laces, though a decade later, bobbin laces would attempt to imitate flat Venetian.

*Charles-Louis and Robert de Bavière*, Antony Van Dyck.
*c.* 1645
Oil on canvas
Paris, Musée du Louvre

The two young men wear collars bordered with needle lace patterned with naturalistic flowers, after designs by Danieli

Edge of a collar. Bobbins. 'Passement'. Flanders or Spain, *c.* 1635
Linen 10 × 32 cm
Lyons, Musée Historique des Tissus

Note the stylized tulips at the base of the scallops

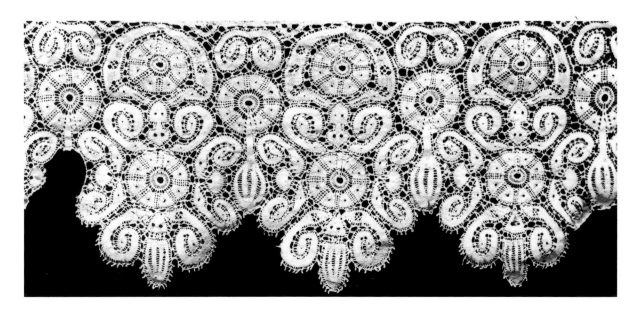

*Nicolas de l'Hôpital, duc de Vitry*, French school, seventeenth century, *c.* 1645
Oil on canvas
Versailles, Musée National du Château et des Trianons

The duke's collar is edged with a wide bobbin lace decorated with stylized flowers. It is worn on ceremonial armour blazoned with trophies of war

Pages 40–41
*The marriage of Willem Van Loon and Margaretha Bas*, Jan Miense Molenaet, 1637
Oil on canvas
Amsterdam, Van Loon Foundation

This painting forms an anthology of fashion towards the middle of the seventeenth century, particularly of lace fashion. All the people represented, except the servants, wear laces of linen thread, as well as gold and silver. Notice that most of the men wear large flat collars of needle lace while the women wear two-layered collars, almost like fichus, of bobbin lace. The records of the time indicate that needle lace collars were often much more expensive than those of bobbin lace. The men, therefore, are more richly dressed here than the women. The mother of the little girl wears no lace, either on her collar or her cuffs. Her short coat and the seams and hem of her skirt are however trimmed with a narrow lace, altogether much less spectacular than that of her husband, whose hand she holds

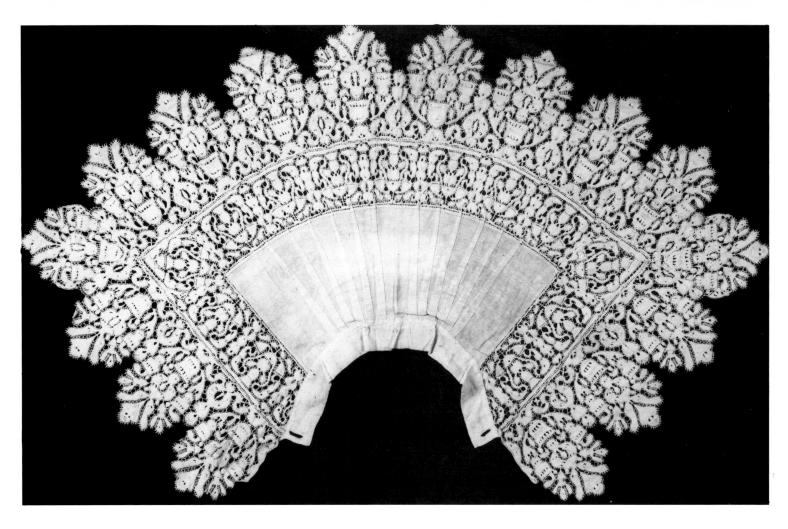

Man's collar. Bobbin.
'Passements'. Flanders,
Antwerp region, *c.* 1635
Linen, middle height 38 cm
Ecouen, Musée National de
la Renaissance; inv. Cl.
17046

Van Dyck collar with
motifs of vases of stylized
tulips along the inner and
outer borders. The woven
linen with twelve pleats
forming the centre is
original. Note the two
buttonholes through which
a cord ending in tassels
would be passed, to tie
beneath the chin

For the time being, Flemish laces were
particularly well adapted to the demands of
fashion. Their lovely soft linen, of a pearly
whiteness, contrasted in a striking fashion with
the often sombre-coloured clothing of the
period, and with armour. Masculine elegance
decreed magnificent laces on armour. The most
severe militia, and the least suspect of ambigu-
ity, posed unhesitatingly for their portraits with
great collars of lace advantageously displayed
over breastplates of burnished steel.

Among civilians, the masculine shirt became
voluminous in the 1630s, and called for deep
cuffs of lace which concealed half the hands.
The tops of the boots, widely folded back, were
lined with lace. The shoulder-belt was fringed
with gold lace, as were the gloves, the canions
and the shoe-roses. The seams of the knee-
breeches and justaucorps (a fitted coat) were
emphasized with gold or silver lace.

As for the children, they wore as much lace as
adults. Little boys and little girls alike wore
gowns, bonnets and aprons trimmed with a
profusion of lace. There was no difference at all
between the clothes of the two sexes up to the
age of seven years.

Paradoxically, it was women who wore less
lace during the period from 1630 to 1650. A
large collar of plain white linen, edged with lace,
or a sort of lace bertha around the shoulders,
with matching cuffs, often constituted their
only finery, especially after marriage.

It was at this time that a lace appeared on the
market which was totally original: Venetian gros
point. Immediately it was all the fashion. Its
great novelty was the introduction of relief –
obtained by emphasizing certain motifs with a
core of thick threads oversewn with buttonhole
stitches, which gave it a truly sculptural quality.
As for the flat areas of the design, they were
embellished with all kinds of decorative stitches
– chevrons, diamond-shaped panes, stripes,
holes, point d'esprit – and these the bobbin laces
were soon to transpose into their own techniques. However the strong relief from which
the gros point took its name could not be copied
by a bobbin lace technique, and it was this
which made gros point impossible to imitate,
and hence so successful. Venetian lacemakers,
perhaps at first frightened of the freedom their
technique of 'stitches in the air' permitted them,
had been slow to break free of the aesthetic

Rabat. Needle. 'Venetian gros point'. Probably French, Royal manufactory (?), 1665 to 1670
Linen 15 × 78 cm
Paris, Musée des Arts Décoratifs; inv. 21423

The beautiful arrangement of the collar around a central axis and the perfect equilibrium of its proportions indicate without any doubt a French origin. Note the abundance of little 'buttons' embroidered on the motifs

43

Flounce (detail). Bobbins
and needle. 'Venetian gros
point'. Flanders, *c.* 1670
Linen 35 × 190 cm
Italy, private collection

This piece is an example of
the exceptional quality of
the attempts made in the
seventeenth century to
imitate Venetian gros point.
Here most of the motifs are
worked with bobbins,
which is quicker and less
expensive than with the
needle. The raised parts are
made with a cordonnet in
the classic needle-lace style.
The very even clothstitch
of the bobbin areas, the
central motif of a huge
stylized tulip, the slightly
naive character of the
whole, as opposed to the
sensual sophistication of
Venice, indicates a Flanders
production. It is however
almost certain that
imitations of gros point
were also made in Italy

*The Duchess of Orléans with
her children* (detail), Jean
Murat. *c.* 1680. Copy
(1837) of the original
Oil on canvas
Versailles, Musée National
du Château et des Trianons

The little boy, the future
regent of France, is still
dressed as a girl. He would
therefore be between six
and seven years old. He
wears a cap, stomacher,
cuffs and an apron trimmed
with Venetian gros point

44

notions that had prevailed at the time of their discovery; but around 1650 the Baroque style of more expressive shapes with vigorous contours, long current in sculpture, had reached the decorative arts. Inspired both by this trend and by various oriental influences, Venetian lacemakers succeeded in developing an entirely new style in just a few years.

From the Baroque, Venetian gros point borrowed its bold contours, its sense of perspective and its rhythmic strength; from the East, the repetition of a strictly plant-like decorative theme, the *leitmotif* of which was the pomegranate. Instead of human figures or stylized animals or crystalline shapes, the design was an ensemble of broad scrolls punctuated by finials along a continuous path, the whole producing a sensual effect of movement far removed from the static compartmentalism of the preceding laces. The elements were linked together, where the design left spaces, by straight buttonhole-stitched bars, often embellished at their mid-points with starry picots.

This heavy lace sat especially well on men, and they adopted it without restraint. The col rabat, made fashionable by the young Louis XIV, who was crowned King of France in 1654, was made of two rectangles of gros point knotted under the chin with tassels of braid, or held together by a bow-tie. With the rabat were worn matching cuffs, but also the rhingrave, a short skirt-like band of lace hiding the lower part of the petticoat-breeches, and in addition canions which formed a little collar around each knee, forcing men to walk with their legs apart. In vain ferocious satires of the period scoffed at this extravagant fashion: 'one cannot enter the presence of the King without Venetian lace', as a character in a contemporary play remarked.

The ladies of the court adapted the masculine style of gros point to their own use very well. They wore it as berthas around their shoulders or as head-dresses. Their skirts were pulled back at the sides to allow petticoats made entirely of gros point to be displayed. Gros

point was also used in furnishings, and the inventory of the Royal goods in 1667 notes that the alcove curtains of the pleasure barques in which the King sailed on the grand canal at Versailles were of Venetian gros point.

The outlay necessary for the importation of these laces, of which the most beautiful could only be obtained from Venice, must have been enormous. Precise and reliable figures of expenditure are difficult to trace for the period, and a more complete study remains to be done on this subject. However, the sums were sufficiently large to attract the attention of the Minister of Finance and Trade to Louis XIV, Jean-Baptiste Colbert. He understood at once that the solution lay not in restrictions on wearing lace, which had been many times renewed and always ignored, but in the establishment of a local industry.

The first half of the century had been a very

disturbed period for France, and she had fallen behind, particularly in comparison with her Flemish and Italian neighbours, in the development of manufacturing industries, notably in the production of fabrics, tapestries, glass and lace. While the lace industry existed in France on a large scale, as previously mentioned, it was geographically dispersed, badly structured commercially, and above all it had no clearly defined style. This situation was of a kind which stimulated Colbert's organizational and reforming capacities. His first care was that the King should sign a decree establishing Royal manufacturies of lace in a number of towns, granting them a subsidy and naming as their heads administrators chosen by Colbert himself.

This proclamation was published on 5 August 1665, and stipulated that there should be created 'in the towns of Quesnoy, Arras, Rheims, Sedan, Château-Thierry, Loudun, Alençon, Aurillac and others of the kingdom, factories for all kinds of threadwork made either with the needle or on the cushion, in the manner of laces which were made in Venice, in Genoa ... and other foreign countries, and which would be called Points de France'. In order that the laces manufactured in these workshops would be 'as rich and as perfect' as those made in Venice and Flanders, Colbert proposed to send for some thirty of the best workers from Venice and two hundred from Flanders. It was hoped that these would assist the French to master the ultimate technical perfections, and to acquire that professionalism which they had hitherto lacked. In the event, Colbert never succeeded in attracting such a large number of qualified persons, despite the offer made to them of immediately obtaining French nationality.

There were at that time a very large number of foreign craftsmen and artists in every part of France – not a state of affairs to please their countries of origin. The Venetian Senate in particular did not appreciate this call to workers to emigrate – master-weavers and glassmakers were similarly being enticed away – and by

*Portrait, probably of the Princesse des Ursins*, French school, *c.* 1670
Oil on canvas
Chantilly, Musée Condé

The princess wears a hooded cloak of Venetian gros point, matching her cuffs and tippet. The scarf of brocaded gauze on her head seems intended to offset by its lightness the slight heaviness of the gros point around her face

decree they commanded those who were tempted to depart not to do so. They warned those who had already responded to foreign offers to return, under pain of 'being executed as traitors to their country'. One understands why, under such circumstances, letters from Colbert to the French ambassador in Venice, Cardinal Bonzy, were often written in number code. At times when they were not, one can read that the Cardinal obtained information on the Venetian lace industry through trustworthy friends in the town. He quoted figures for levels of production and the price of laces. He gave details of the organization of the manufacture, and of its sales. In short, he practised industrial espionage. This work bore fruit, since from their beginning the Royal French manufacturies set themselves to produce only copies of Venetian gros point, and it is indeed difficult to distinguish French needle laces of the years 1660 to 1670 from their Venetian models. Neither the technique nor the thread used can help us, because they are exactly the same. The only difference to be discerned is perhaps in the aesthetic approach. The tactile sensual appeal of the Venetian scroll ornaments, studded rather at random with heavy flowers and bursting pomegranates, were foreign to French taste which favoured more austere and disciplined ornamentation. While the Venetian designs were nearly always disposed along the length of the lace, the decoration of the French gros points was arranged depthwise, with flowers and pomegranates equally distributed on either side of a median axis. The whole already carried the imprint of French classicism.

Colbert's idea, however, was not just to make Venetian lace in France, it was to make French lace. He understood that markets were conquered not with copies, but with new products. He therefore asked the King's appointed painters and designers to contribute their ideas. The designs for use by the manufacturers came only from Paris, and no laceworker or merchant outside the Royal manufactures was allowed to copy them. This strategy of centralization encountered plenty of opposition. The inhabitants of the towns were reluctant to send their daughters into apprenticeship at the factories. Colbert repeatedly threatened them with severe punishments if they did not, and offered the inducement of exemption from the obligation to take in soldiers, then current, if they complied.

Independent workers rebelled against the manufactures, without whose mediation they were forbidden to sell their goods. The monopoly of manufacture provoked riots, notably in Alençon; and frauds were numerous. The convents in particular, where the state could not enter, continued to make lace independently and to sell it.

In spite of these difficulties, or perhaps even because of them, the French lace industry succeeded, in less than ten years, in establishing a name for itself and in producing work which was instantly recognizable, in both style and technique, as French lace. Even after the cessation, in 1675, of the subsidies initially granted for nine years to the manufactures, some among them, notably Alençon and Sedan, continued to produce spectacular pieces, a considerable number of which survive.

In the 1670s point de France established its ascendancy because, like the Venetian gros point before it, it was completely new. To give point de France its distinctive appearance the French lacemakers first of all totally eliminated the high relief of the Venetian laces, while preserving the raised technique to give a more discreet emphasis to the units of the design. Next they created what constitutes the principal characteristic of point de France, a network of large hexagonal meshes covered with close buttonhole stitches and decorated with picots on all their sides. This network of meshes forms a veritable grid on which the well-ordered designs preferred by French taste could be displayed with a severe and classic elegance that Italy and Flanders would attempt to imitate, but without ever wholly succeeding. From around 1670 to 1690, the decoration of the wide point de France flounces shows the influence of Charles le Brun, painter to the King from 1662 and director of the 'Manufacture des Gobelins et de Mobilier Royal' (the Gobelins Tapestries and Royal Furniture Manufactures). This was not exceptional: all the decorative arts of the period were consistent, in spirit and proportions, with the style of the French court. The designs used for laces correspond therefore with those of furniture inlaid with wood or metal, the carved panelling and the wrought iron of the palace of Versailles. Firstly, there are numerous allusions to Louis XIV; suns, sunflowers, fleur-de-lys or crowns, even the likeness of the King himself as a Roman emperor. Later, when the

Furnishing flounce (detail). Needle. 'Point de France'. France, Royal manufactory (?), 1670–85
Linen 62 × 330 cm
Paris, Musée des Arts Décoratifs; inv. 52847B

The central vase, with handles and pedestal, holds a sunflower. Another open sunflower is found, oddly, upside down below the vase. The sunflower is an allusion to Louis XIV. Its presence here indicates a royal commission, for the King's personal use, or more probably a present for him to give to a member of his court
Green silk: Maud Perle, Paris

France worth 18,491 *livres* at the Royal manufacturies. In comparison, the annual salary of Charles le Brun was 11,200 *livres*. A piece of furniture by André-Charles Boulle, the most celebrated cabinet-maker of his time, was valued at some 8,000 *livres*, and the portrait of the Queen Mother Anne of Austria painted by Beaubrun cost only 750 *livres*. It should be added that Beaubrun wrote a letter to Colbert, on the subject of this portrait, complaining that he had received less from the King than from his private clients. One can imagine that this painter, although very highly regarded at the time, did not wear much point de France.

In spite of its high price, the success of point de France was so rapid and so complete that even Venetians 'did not feel properly attired without it', according to a contemporary writer. The inventory of a merchant of Venetian laces, dated 1671, confirms its popularity: seven years after the opening of the French Royal manufacturies it includes laces *alla Colberta* which were among the most expensive in the shop.

The more and more numerous proclamations which the commercial authorities of Venice published against the importation of foreign laces, from the 1670s, show clearly that the situation of the lace industry in the city had deteriorated not only in comparison with that of France, but also with that of Flanders. Venetian lacemakers were reduced to making copies of point de France, or to exaggerating their technical virtuosity to the detriment of the design in the effort to make their production distinctive. Point de neige, which appeared around 1680, was the last original Venetian lace. It was a needle lace characterized by very small motifs, their outlines overloaded with picots. This superposition of minuscule elements gave the lace a snow-like appearance from which it derived its name. The excesses which this technique favoured ended by making the motifs almost indistinguishable. These laces remain, none the less, one of the most spectacular and

splendour of the French monarchy declined, these allusions gave way to more purely decorative elements: large vases such as those in the park at Versailles, consoles, pyramids of fruit, musicians or dancers, or even American Indians with feathered head-dresses.

Plenty of space was needed for such compositions to be shown to their best advantage, and this was achieved most easily on the long deep flounces which were mainly used in furnishing such as the fittings of a dressing-table, or on the albs of church dignitaries. These large pieces were expensive. It is known that in the single month of July 1666, Louis XIV bought point de

one of the most inimitable examples of the lacemaker's skill.

If, however, Venetian lace temporarily regained the advantage, it was because the revocation of the edict of Nantes in 1685 struck a heavy blow to the French industry, especially in Normandy, where many Protestants who had worked at lace were forced to disperse to other parts of Europe. The population of lacemakers in this region was reduced by half, a situation which profited not only Venice but also Flanders. In the last years of the century bobbin laces regained all the ground which point de France had caused them to lose. Flemish lacemakers had been obliged to imitate point de France, and had succeeded in transposing into their technique the varied decorative stitches developed for needle lace. Above all, they had perfected a method which enabled them to create the very deep flounces which point de France had made fashionable. This was the

non-continuous-thread technique (*à pièces rapportées*). It consisted in making the design-motifs first, then joining them with a network or *réseau* of plaited meshes. The ground threads required to make the network were obtained by taking sewings (using needle or hook) around the outside of the motifs. This system allowed several people to work at the same time on one flounce, which could be of unlimited size. The designs of these laces were inspired at first by Italian needle lace patterns – broad scrolls, florets like fleur-de-lys, pomegranates – then by those of the painted and printed fabrics imported into Europe from India in large quantities despite prohibitions. As with all the improvements in technique, the non-continuous-thread method was rapidly made use of everywhere, and in particular in Italy, where at this time historians traditionally associate it with the region of Milan. In fact, the Milanese lace industry was probably never so important as the number of laces attributed to it would suggest. The archives of the town contain little more than a trace of the industry, whereas the Venetian archives contain a comparatively large quantity of documents. Many of the laces attributed to Milan were doubtless made in Venice and its environs.

In France, at the end of the seventeenth century, bobbin laces continued to be made in Normandy and elsewhere in the north. Even non-continuous-thread laces were made, although that was prohibited in France. Officially, the reason for the prohibition was that these laces were of inferior quality: they were weaker because they were made of separate parts. But in reality the French authorities were seeking to discredit laces which were now much sought after to the detriment of the needle laces in which France excelled. It should be emphasized that despite the large quantities of bobbin laces made in France since the sixteenth century, it was only in the mid-eighteenth century that French lacemakers were able at last, with Valenciennes, to compete seriously with Flemish lacemakers in the production of bobbin laces. Indeed, the exemplary success of the needle laces was difficult to equal, for the big flounces of point de France from the years 1670 to 1690 represent a particularly apt expression of the French taste of the period, characterized at its best by a severe elegance from which facility of composition was banished.

Steinkerque

D. de Flandre

D. de Hol...

D. de Maline

Rabois

Dantelle
du Havre

Linon

# The great laces of the seventeenth century and their characteristics

## VENETIAN

### Point plat (flat Venetian)

A needle lace, made between 1630 and 1650, in which the motifs are formed of thin strands of uniform width, worked flat, then joined by straight bars oversewn with buttonhole stitches, or sometimes made with bobbins. Its decoration still shows a tendency towards the compartmentalism inherited from the geometric designs of the previous century. It is sometimes difficult with the naked eye to distinguish these laces from those of similar design made with bobbins.

### Venetian gros point

A needle lace the designs of which are completely free of all technical constraint. The strong relief of gros point is obtained by positioning a strand of about fifty threads around the borders of certain motifs, fixing it at its two ends on the same motif, then covering it with compact buttonhole stitches, and picots. In contrast to the preceding lace, the solid areas are worked with decorative stitches which contribute to the raised effect. At first, around 1650 to 1660, the motifs were simply sewn together in such a way as to leave the spaces completely open, which increased the relief effect of the whole. Then, from about 1660, the motifs were linked by crowned and picoted brides which became more and more numerous, a multiplicity which foreshadowed the network of meshes of both bobbin and needle laces at the end of the century. This immensely successful gros point gave rise to many copies, such as those of the French

Collar edging (detail). Needle. 'Venetian point plat'. Germany or Austria (?), c. 1650
Linen 9 × 56 cm
Paris, private collection

Notice the two-headed eagle, rather naively treated, at the centre of each fleuron. This eagle, which appears in the arms of the house of Austria, suggests that it is not Italian work, because at that time none of the Italian provinces was under Austrian domination

Below:
Flounce (detail). Needle. 'Venetian gros point'. Italy, 1660–80 (?)
Linen 16 × 180 cm
Paris, private collection

This flounce is made up of various fragments of the same period. Certain parts of the design are emphasized by a twisted or interlaced cord rather than by a true cordonnet. It is another form of imitation Venetian gros point

Page 54
*Habit de lingère* (Clothes of the linen-merchant), engraving by Nicolas de l'Armessin. 1695
Paris, Bibliothèque Nationale

This engraving is interesting for the names of different laces that are shown. The bodice 'with drawers' bears the following labels: Flanders lace, Dutch lace, Mechlin, Rabats. On the table is a Le Havre lace

Flounce (detail). Needle.
'Venetian rose point'.
Venice, c. 1685
Linen 17 × 100 cm
Florence, Palazzo
Davanzati; inv. Stoffe 1395

The decoration of foliated
scrolls punctuated by
flowers is treated in the
horizontal, which appears
to be a distinctive feature
of Italian productions.
Another is the slightly
haphazard spatial
distribution of the design
elements

Royal manufacturies. Because it was slow and difficult to make, attempts were made to achieve the same effect by more rapid means. The solid areas, for example, might be made with bobbins, or by using woven tapes; the cordonnet (*la brode*) was replaced by a simple cord sewn around the motifs, etc. These contemporary imitations were certainly not as technically refined as gros point, but they nevertheless had the especial charm possessed by all attempts to produce beautiful objects with restricted means.

### Rose point

This term dates from the nineteenth century. It applies to a type of Venetian lace similar to the earlier gros point in its design, but with a less heavy outline, sometimes even with no outline at all, and much smaller motifs. It is hard to see why the name was invented, unless because of the love of the picturesque which characterized all later names. It is often used in nineteenth-century texts to describe laces of the eighteenth century, and so must be included here.

### Point de neige

A needle lace where there is not a cordonnet, strictly speaking, but an accumulation of picots, themselves in turn picoted. The motifs are minute. The design consists for the most part of vermiculate scrolls, with sometimes, especially in French forms, the addition of allegorical personages or mythical animals. Its name, like that of rose point above, is late. Point de neige should not be confused with the decorative stitch in the form of small circles which is called fond de neige in bobbin laces.

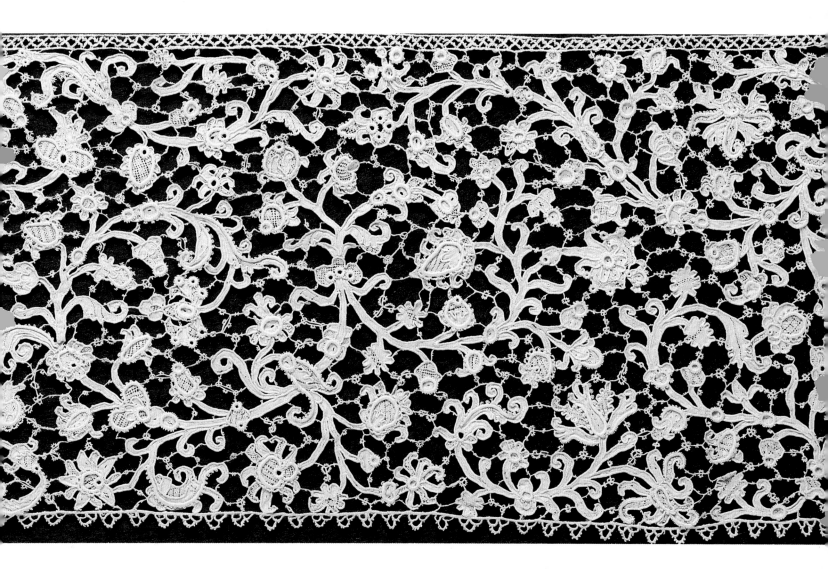

## Point de France

The technical characteristics of point de France are as follows: it is a needle lace with closely worked motifs, using both simple and fancy stitches; a meshwork of brides joined together in such a way as to form real meshes of hexagonal form, covered with buttonhole stitches and picoted on four sides. This type of network or *réseau*, invented by French lacemakers, appeared around 1670. The cordonnet is made of a strand of threads as in gros point, but much thinner. Point de France, as described here, appears to have been perfected by the lacemakers of Alençon, but of course the other Royal manufactures also made it. Nevertheless there is general agreement that the best flounces, with designs obviously created by first-rate artists, could not have been carried out except in Alençon, Argentan or Sedan.

These are the only towns where the needle lace industry existed before the Royal manufactures were set up, and where it survived and prospered after their cessation as state enterprises.

## BOBBIN LACES

### Genoa

Genoese lace is a continuous-thread lace; its decorations always consist of rosettes, shells and stylized carnations often worked in point d'esprit. It was highly prized at the beginning of the seventeenth century, but the fashion had passed by 1650. However the production of Genoese lace never completely ceased, and it was still made in the Ligurian countryside at the beginning of the twentieth century. The designs of Le Puy lace owe their inspiration to it.

### Flanders/Angleterre

The two terms were used without distinction in the seventeenth century to designate a bobbin lace made by the non-continuous-thread technique. The exotic flowers and characteristic foliated scrolls of the designs unfurled on a ground of plaited brides (sometimes made with a needle) or on a network of meshes plaited on all sides and worked parallel to the footing. The 'five-hole' ground with its big round meshes was one of the numerous variants which occurred most frequently. Aesthetically this kind of lace was perfected around 1650, and its designs, then, were inspired by Venetian needle laces. Towards the end of the century designs became more vermiculate, in imitation of point de France; or on the other hand more exotic, in the style of painted fabrics from Persia or India. The production

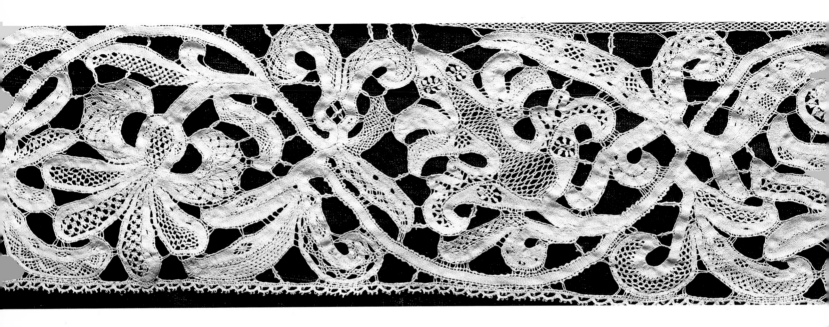

Above:
Flounce (detail). Bobbin
lace. 'Flanders'. Flanders,
c. 1680
Linen 14 × 230 cm
Italy, private collection

Design of carnations and
stylized tulips worked in a
great variety of decorative
stitches
Green silk: Maud Perle,
Paris

Flounce (detail). Bobbin
lace. 'Flanders'. Flanders or
Italy, c. 1680
Linen
West Berlin,
Kunstgewerbemuseum

Note the almost total
absence of bars. The
resultant open effect
illustrates very effectively
the central idea of lace, that
is, the alternation of solid
design areas and open
spaces. The somewhat
gauche treatment indicates
a provincial work

of Flanders laces continued at a crafts level and without great technical or stylistic changes during the whole of the nineteenth century and up to the Second World War, not only in Flanders but generally. Except where regional or national characteristics asserted themselves sufficiently for clear differentiations of style to be seen, that is, essentially from the end of the seventeenth and early eighteenth century, it is difficult to pinpoint the exact area of production of so-called Flanders laces, since all the peasant areas of Europe were making them.

The trade designation 'Angleterre' of these laces probably arose from their original prohibition. Merchants had them transported via England, where there were numerous customers for this merchandise, before smuggling them into French territory. The sea route was apparently better for this clandestine importation than the large road networks between Flanders and France, punctuated as they were with city tolls. It is unlikely that this practice could be carried on for very long because the sumptuary and commercial laws of the English also forbade the entry and transport of lace. In fact it probably only occurred at the beginning of its production, but the name 'Angleterre' remained attached to Flemish laces, particularly those of Brussels. One thing is certain: despite their name, England never made them.

*Milan*

Milanese lace is a non-continuous-thread bobbin lace, exactly similar technically to the lace of Flanders described above. The laces were often made of a tape-like strip worked with

bobbins, or this strip might sometimes simply be folded and stitched around the outlines of the design. The ground is composed of straight plaited brides, or of large meshes plaited on all sides. The criteria which allow a distinction to be made between the laces of Milan and those of Flanders are not established with certainty. Some authors think that the ground meshes of Milan are made in all directions around the motifs rather than in a lengthwise direction. In this way the Milanese lacemakers could avoid the necessity of passing the threads under the motifs on the reverse side, as was done in Flemish laces. But possibly designs, rather than a specific technique, may be attributed to Italy, or even to Milan, for a technique can more readily be exported than a style. Italian productions of the seventeenth century and early eighteenth century are always more or less inspired by the designs of Venetian gros point. As with Flanders, the productions of Milan continued throughout peasant Europe until the beginning of the twentieth century.

59

Below:
Chalice veil. Needle.
'Venetian point plat'. Italy,
1630–50
Gold or silver metal
threads, polychrome silks
75 × 75 cm
Private collection, formerly
Spink & Sons, London

Four stems of fleur-de-lys,
symbol of the Virgin, form
the cornerpieces. In

contrast to the previous
illustration, the design
elements stand out clearly
against a sparse ground of
simple bars, the colour
giving sharp emphasis to
their rounded contours

Bed- or table-cover (detail).
Needle. 'Venetian point
plat'. Eastern Europe or
Spain (?) c. 1645
Gold or silver metal
threads, polychrome silk
172 × 136 cm
Los Angeles County
Museum of Art; inv.
M.87.112.6

The shading of the stylized
tulip where the central row

is worked in a darker silk,
the rustic character of the
design, the method of
working – in a continuous
course – so that no part of
the design is detached from
any other either physically
or aesthetically, indicates a
provincial or foreign work,
perhaps from Russia or
Hungary, although similar
pieces have also been
attributed to Spain

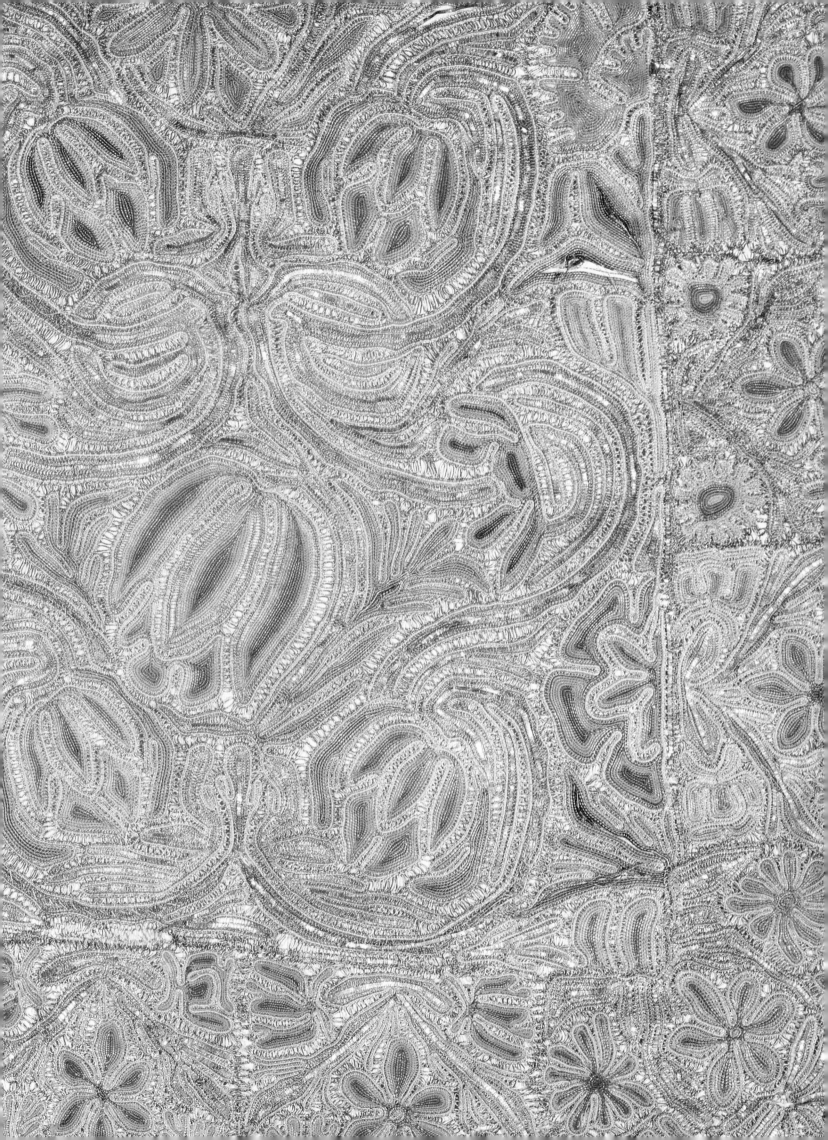

Bed-cover said to have belonged to Marie-Thérèse. Needle. 'Venetian point plat'. Worked in a French or Spanish convent, 1660–80
Linen 190 × 253 cm
Versailles, Musée National du Château et des Trianons

As far as we know, no other lace exists in France of equal historic or artistic importance. Even though precise records concerning this piece have not been found, at least up to the present time, in the Royal wardrobe accounts, there is little doubt – given its design – that it belonged to the French royal family. The central motif shows the coat of arms of France and Navarre surmounted by a royal crown encircled with crowned Ls (the monogram of Louis XIV) and with fleur-de-lys. Moving further outwards, the initials of the King are intertwined with those of his wife, Marie-Thérèse of Austria, within a laurel wreath. In addition to numerous heraldic figures and the coats of arms of the most important European nobility, there are figures of

women representing the four cardinal virtues – Prudence, Justice, Temperance and Strength – as well as of Ceres, the goddess of harvest. These figures are dressed in the fashion of the 1670s, with panniered gowns of banded effect, and their hair in ringlets. Notice the printed appearance of the clothes of the central angels, with the flower motifs among the stripes. The extreme diversity of stitches, the pursuit of a variegated effect, rayed and partitioned, perhaps indicates a Flemish or Spanish origin rather than a French. The very archaic style, where all the decorative elements are given an equivalent spatial value, the traditionalism of the showing of the coats of arms, and the numerous symbols, are the marks of a commissioned work, made in a convent for example, rather than in the workshop of a lace manufacturer. For a more complete description of this piece, see no. 20 in the catalogue of the Lyons exhibition (Bibliography)

Cravat-end, possibly of Louis XIV. Bobbin lace. 'Brussels, called point d'Angleterre'. Brussels, 1675–1715
Linen 31 × 40 cm
London, collection Spink & Sons

It is not impossible that this cravat should have belonged to Louis XIV. The design includes many allusions to the King and to a military victory which could be that of the crossing of the Rhine in 1672, during the war between France and the United Provinces. In addition to the trophies of war – drums, standards, weapons – there are two angels blowing the trumpets of fame and supporting a dais on which is perched the cock of France. The sun, emblem of Louis XIV, appears to smile at the angel on the right, out of clouds and shafts of lightning, symbolizing the return of peace. Finally, in the middle of the border appears the monogram of Louis XIV, the double L. The other end of this cravat is now at the Art Institute of Chicago. This piece is the subject of a forthcoming article by the author

Furnishing flounce. Needle lace. 'Point de Sedan'. France, Royal manufactory (?), perhaps Sedan, *c.* 1680
Linen 65 × 305 cm
Paris, Musée des Arts Décoratifs; inv. 55854. Formerly collection of the Prince and Princess de la Tour d'Auvergne-Lauraguais

Here, the richness of decoration, the height of the central vase, the diversity of decorative stitches, and above all the placing of the cordonnet inside the motifs rather than along their contours, all indicate the type of production traditionally associated with Sedan

Flounce (detail). Needle lace. 'Point de France'. France, Royal manufactory (?), possibly Alençon, 1675–85
Linen 38 × 360 cm
Italy, private collection

The design of this piece is strictly symmetrical on either side of a large central vase from which arises a stem of flowers, flanked by cornucopia and naturalistic blooms. The relatively small size of the motifs is perfectly suited to the space occupied by the ground, which forms a clear meshwork. The effect is one of great elegance

Furnishing flounce (detail).
Needle lace. 'Point de
France'. France, Royal
manufactory (?), perhaps
Alençon or Sedan, 1680–
1715
Linen 65 × 300 cm
London, Victoria and
Albert Museum; inv. T
88.1922

The design combines
Baroque and an Indo-
Persian influence, giving
the whole a brilliantly rich
impression far removed
from the French classical
taste, even though the
motifs are arranged in
conformity with the rules
of the period. It is in every
way an ambitious and
outstanding piece which
could only have been
created to special
commission for an
important person. It gave
rise to a number of copies,
both contemporary and
later. A more detailed study
remains to be done on the
sources of inspiration of its
design

Skirt flounce (detail).
Bobbin. 'Brussels'. Brussels, *c.* 1750. Linen 35 × 130
Paris, private collection

This type of flounce was worn gathered or pleated on the lower part of the
skirts of the period. Above it there would be a smaller matching flounce which
would make a heading and also hide the attachment

# THE EIGHTEENTH CENTURY

# FEMININITY

*Portrait of Madame Loys*
François Hubert Drouais, *c.* 1765. Oil on canvas
Paris, Hôtel Matignon (dépôt du Louvre)

Madame Loys wears a complete outfit of Argentan lace in which the large
meshes are clearly seen. Her stomacher is made of seven rows of lace; she
wears pleated quills on either side of it which would descend to the hem of
her gown, a matching stole around her shoulders, and engageantes which are
just visible at the elbow

Page 73
Pair of lappets. Needle.
'Réseau Venise'. Brussels or
Venice, 1700–15
Linen 13 × 103 cm
Florence, Palazzo
Davanzati; G.A.A. 3142–3

The decoration of vases of flowers, cartouches and branches is arranged in 'candelabra', that is, the various equal-sized design elements are placed one above the other. The arrangement is in general typical of the Italian style. In France, on the other hand, although all the motifs might be arranged vertically, their size would increase or decrease along the axis. Belgian productions tended to follow the French, and it seems unlikely that these lappets were made in Brussels, despite the extreme fineness of their thread

Bonnet-back. Needle.
'Réseau Venise'. Venice (?),
*c.* 1720
Linen 22 × 27 cm
Florence, Palazzo
Davanzati; inv. 1423

The design of a rounded vase on a pedestal, from which fall heavy flowers in full bloom, is constructed in a disciplined fashion. The decorative stitches are placed with perfect mastery wherever they will be most effective. By contrast, the small square meshes of the ground lack uniformity, an effect characteristic of the productions of Burano, although pieces of this quality have been attributed by some authors to Brussels. Documents preserved in Venice show that 'superfine' needle laces were made in Venice and Burano throughout the eighteenth century

As far as lace was concerned, the eighteenth century was a time of specialization. The name Brussels (or 'Angleterre') would now be used, also Binche, Mechlin and Valenciennes for bobbin laces, and Alençon, Sedan and Argentan for needle laces. In France, most of the Royal manufactures did not survive the termination of the financial subsidies, except in the regions where the lace industry had not been, as it were, artificially implanted by Colbert. Among these, the regions of Alençon and Argentan were able to retain the prestige which being the seat of a Royal manufactory had brought them, while fending for themselves commercially. Some towns not cited in the decree of 1665, notably Le Puy, continued to maintain their production at a high level, quantitatively speaking, throughout the century, though curiously without their name becoming attached to a well-defined form before the second half of the following century. The same applies to towns such as Rouen or Caen, where it is known that good bobbin laces were produced, since official reports of the Louis XIV period mention the industry there, but without terming them 'Caen' or 'Rouen' laces. The productions of the little towns of the Normandy coast, on the other hand, were sufficiently differentiated for inventories of the time to mention laces of Dieppe, Le Havre, Fécamp or Honfleur. In the north, with the exception of Sedan where lacemakers worked with the needle, bobbin laces were made over

the whole region which had no well-defined characteristics. Valenciennes did not become a French town until 1678, and it was not until the 1740s that its laces became dissociated from those of neighbouring Flanders. Other regions, such as central and eastern France, produced plenty of laces, but they were of mediocre aesthetic quality. All the same they were important because they provided work for many people.

During the whole of the first half of the eighteenth century, so great was the demand for lace that there was room for all kinds, including the simplest. This held true for the whole of Europe, which during the years 1720 to 1760 experienced a population increase and rise in the general standard of living which favoured trade in consumer goods. The sumptuary laws forbidding the wearing of lace to certain classes of society – like the economic conditions which had prevented its purchase by the poorer classes – were no longer operative. Ladies' maids wore as much lace as their mistresses, and peasants put on lace with their Sunday best just like city-dwellers.

This constantly expanding lace market profited above all the Flemish laces, for fashion claimed them. They were very fine and light, which the completely outmoded laces of Venice were not, and more quickly made than the French laces. The Brussels laces (those which were called point d'Angleterre) were worked by the non-continuous-thread technique which allowed very large pieces to be created much more quickly than by the continuous-thread technique or with a needle. Such speed of production meant that the Flemish lacemakers, and in particular those of Brussels, could respond to fluctuations of fashion and immediately offer their clients the latest models. Moreover, the bobbin technique gave the lace a very supple texture, and a light and frothy appearance. Needle lace could never imitate these characteristics: the cordonnet which emphasized its motifs, the meshes of the ground which, being covered with buttonhole stitches, were necessarily more rigid, gave it on the contrary a rather stiff appearance. However, their severe elegance helped to maintain for the French needle productions the position of prestige laces *par excellence*, which explains how they still provided at that time direct or indirect subsistence to several tens of thousands of

people in the regions of Alençon and Argentan, even though the quantities of lace produced were far less considerable than in the centres of bobbin lace production.

More and more laces were needed because they were now worn closely gathered, or even pleated. Lace designs could no longer be read in one direction or the other, nor could any specific representations be recognized. The desired effect was a little like the frosting on a cake: the white parts did not entirely obscure the background but allowed it to be glimpsed through their translucency. It should be remembered that the clothes of the first half of the eighteenth century were made in fabrics of particularly striking colours, often abundantly heightened with gold and silver. The white laces served to tone down what might otherwise have appeared rather gaudy, and at the same time provided a contrast which set off these rich fabrics in a particularly happy manner. Lace was not yet worn on underwear; that would come much later, towards the end of the century. For the moment, it was made to be seen. And for the first time, women wore much more lace than men. Their head-pieces were entirely of lace: a pleated edging was set at the front as two arcs joined like the wings of a butterfly; the bonnet-back in matching lace was round, and included a little frill at the base; beneath this frill were attached the lappets. The lappets were two long rectangles of lace which during the last years of the reign of Louis XIV had been allowed to hang freely on the shoulders. In the courts of the eighteenth century, on the contrary, they were most often worn in a loop (*en coque*), that is to say, drawn to the top of the head and held there by a pin or a jewel. Very numerous examples of these eighteenth-century lappets survive today, in public and private collections, and this allows us to appreciate their marvellous designs and skilful arrangements, created in threads of gossamer fineness, where it is hard to say which is the more admirable, the perfect mastery of the technique or the beauty of the design. This could scarcely be observed at the time because the laces were never worn flat.

The engageantes, or ladies' ruffles, were worn in three or even four layers. They consisted of frills often specially shaped for their purpose, much wider in the centre than on the sides because, to appear elegant, they needed to be longer at the back than in the front. To obtain

*The Emperor Francis I, the Empress Maria Theresa and their children in 1756* (detail), after Martin Van Mytens
Oil on canvas
Versailles, Musée National du Château et des Trianons

The Emperor of Austria, father of Marie-Antoinette, wears a cravat and cuffs of needle lace of Argentan/Alençon type. His cloak, coat and breeches are decorated with wide edgings of gold lace, piped and gathered, which contrast oddly with his 'bourgeois' shoes in black leather with their plain studded buckles. His daughter wears six rows of needle lace along her upper arm, an indication of her rank. She also wears a flat flounce around the décolletage of her bodice, while above, a pair of lappets in matching lace fall over her shoulders. Her small sister wears a sleeved cape in blonde with silver thread

this width without incurring the considerable expense of a pair of shaped engageantes, a straight piece of edging could be mounted on a less costly lace which increased in depth at the centre, and would scarcely be seen because of the three or four frills which would overlap it. This cheaper lace was called marli; its designs were usually reduced to a minimum: several trefoils or quatrefoils surrounded by fancy mesh effects. Despite its utilitarian function, marli is clearly visible in some portraits of the period.

The neckline of the gowns was always encircled with an upright frill of gathered lace. The stomacher, or bodice front, was often of gold or silver lace. The sides of the bodice and of the gown were emphasized with long frills of lace mounted in regular pleats, descending as far as the hem. These were called 'quills', doubtless because of their shape which was narrower at the top than at the bottom. Finally, the bottom of the skirt was ornamented with a flounce of gathered lace, more or less deep according to the period.

Considering that some four metres of lace were needed for the engageantes alone, the considerable quantities and huge expense which a complete outfit would entail can be appreciated. Some four ells of lace (1 ell is the equivalent of about 1.20 metres) would be needed to make a pair of engageantes. The prices of a single ell of various laces were listed in the accounts of M. Vanot, linen-supplier to Louis XV, for the month of January, 1765: 'superfine needle lace . . . 480 *livres*'; 'superfine Argentan lace . . . 160 *livres*'; 'real Valenciennes . . . 190 *livres*'; 'Mechlin . . . 95 *livres*'; 'Angleterre . . . 230 *livres*'. A pair of engageantes therefore, made for example in Valenciennes, would cost a total of 760 *livres*. By comparison, the average annual earnings of a Valenciennes lacemaker of the same year was 156 *livres*, less than the cost of a single ell of her own lace.

Dressing-tables, as in the preceding century, were covered with lace, as were peignoirs – the little capes which covered the shoulders while

Lappet, one of a pair (detail)
Bobbin. 'Mechlin'.
Mechlin, *c.* 1740
Linen 10 × 57 cm
Florence, Palazzo Davanzati; inv. Stoffe 1353; cat. no. 497

Note the blending of naturalistic and imaginary flowers of exotic inspiration, as well as the presence of the quatrefoil motif characteristic of Mechlin laces

Stomacher. Needle. 'Point
de France'.
Alençon/Argentan, *c.* 1735
Linen 89 × 116 cm
Paris, private collection

This piece has been cut
from a flounce of point de
France decorated with
vases and large flowers in
such a way that the central
motif appears in the middle
of the stomacher. In the
eighteenth century, with
the exception of some
engageantes and lappets,
the pieces were never made
in the shape required. They
were cut, often less
carefully than here, from
straight flounces, more or
less deep, and put together
with seams, more or less
visible

*Isabella of Parma at the age
of eight years* (detail), Jean-
Marc Nattier, 1749
Oil on canvas
Versailles, Musée National
du Château et des Trianons

The little princess wears a
stomacher and apron of
point de France, cut from a
large flounce perhaps
several years earlier than
her dress. The decoration
of the lace is much heavier
than that of the cloth. A
dressing-table flounce
might, for example, be put
to this use; laces were never
an integral part of dress at
this period, they could
perfectly well be used for
furnishing in the first place
and then for clothing, or
vice versa. Notice also the
draped flounces with
blonde in gold thread at the
hem of her skirt

*Cardinal de la Rochefoucauld, Archbishop of Rouen*, François-Hubert Drouais, *c.* 1745
Oil on canvas
Clermont-Ferrand, Musée-Château de Parentignat

The Cardinal wears a superb alb flounce in needle-made point de France, or Argentan. It is not improbable that at the end of the Cardinal's ecclesiastical career this flounce would have been turned into a trimming for a dressing-table . . .

Below:
Bonnet-back and trimming. Bobbin. 'Brussels, called point d'Angleterre'. Brussels, 1740–50
Linen bonnet, height 18 cm; flounce 7 × 80 cm
Kyoto Costume Institute; inv. 86–13–5 AB

Notice the little Chinese pagodas in the central area of the trimming

the hair was dressed – and what were called *déshabillés*, in fact morning gowns. Since ladies received a great deal in the bedroom, or the dressing-room, it is not surprising that the laces were as abundant in these as in the drawing-rooms. On the other hand, in the intimate situations of which the engravings of the period made a speciality, lace played no part. Eroticism was not in the least one of the qualities attributed to it. It remained above all the symbol of class which it had always been.

As for men, they wore much less lace than in the preceding century, but what they did wear

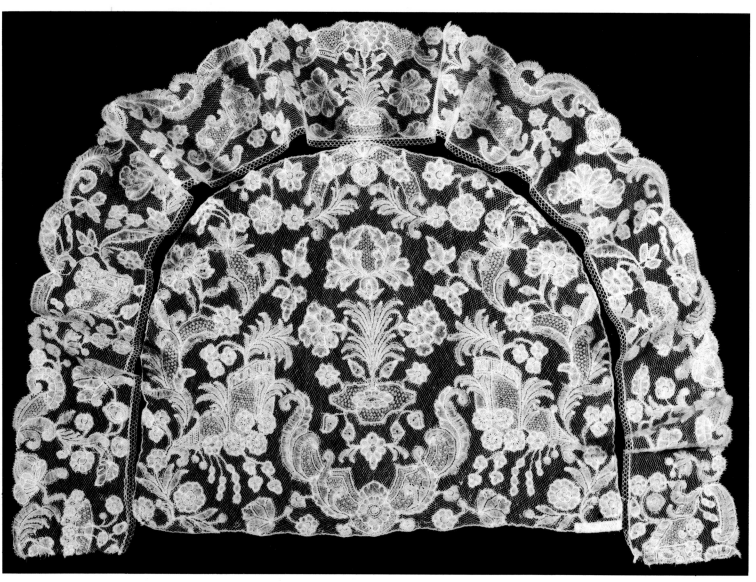

*George Washington* (detail), Adolph Ulrik Wertmüller, Philadelphia, 1795
Oil on canvas
New York, The Metropolitan Museum of Art, bequest of Charles Allen Munn, 1924

The first President of the United States wears a shirt with a jabot of Alençon lace. It is the only known portrait of the President with lace

Previous page:
*Queen Charlotte at her dressing-table with the Prince of Wales and the Duke of York* (detail), Johann Zoffany, *c.* 1764
Oil on canvas
London, the Royal Collection. Reproduced by gracious permission of Her Majesty Queen Elizabeth II

The dressing-table of the Queen is encircled with a deep flounce of Brussels lace. The top mounting is hidden by another smaller flounce. The mirror is draped with two large flounces of the same lace, joined at the top with a bow of salmon-pink watered silk. The triple engageantes and the trimming of the Queen's décolletage are in Brussels bobbin lace of a similar design. This manner of decorating the dressing-tables was *de rigueur* at that time, and a purchase of a complete set of such trimmings represented a considerable outlay

Page 83
*The Princess of Cardito*, eighteenth-century Italian school, *c.* 1760
Oil on canvas
Florence, collection Massimo Listri

The princess's gown is trimmed with a complete set of Valenciennes, of which the square meshes can be clearly distinguished

was perhaps shown to better advantage. A cravat with lace jabot and matching cuffs were essential accessories for the elegant man of the eighteenth century. During the first half of the century, these were most often made of bobbin laces; during the second half, men wore almost exclusively needle lace. Why was this? Perhaps because the trend from the 1760s, following the publication of the great Encyclopaedia of Diderot and d'Alembert, and the publication of Jean-Jacques Rousseau's novel, *Julie ou la nouvelle Héloïse* (1761), was for men to distance themselves from women in many fields, including dress. To simplify, one could say that the supple, the soft and the smooth became feminine attributes, qualities which while applicable to lace in general, are yet more so to bobbin lace than to needle lace, with its stiffer, more brittle, hence perhaps more masculine appearance.

This tendency to make men's clothes more manly was to increase up to the end of the century, and to become definitive from the first years of the following.

The death of that great arbiter of elegance, Mme de Pompadour, in 1764, signalled the end of an era. Moreover, it coincided with sociological and intellectual upheavals which were alluded to earlier. The Romantic trend in particular, as evidenced by Goethe's work *The Sufferings of Young Werther* (1774), wrought a profound change in fashion. It was a time of simplicity. Woman was no longer a luxurious doll, often of easy virtue, but on the contrary a model of purity and delicacy. It was suitable that she should now wear white clothing of a very light texture. This change did not of course happen overnight. In France, Louis XVI and Marie-Antoinette, during the first years of their

FESTINA LENTE

A Sua Eccelenza
La Sig.ra D. Eleonora Savari
Principessa di Cardit...
Napo...

Front of robe. Bobbin.
'Brussels, called point
d'Angleterre', *c.* 1735
Linen 52 × 144 cm
Paris, Musée des Arts
Décoratifs; inv. 22336

The tapering parts are
intended to be placed on
either side of the
stomacher, the ends being
joined behind the neck. It
may have been made for a
statue of the Virgin or of a
saint. The central motif is a
palm-tree, symbol of
paradise. The rest of the
decoration, in *chinoiserie*
style, is quite simply in the
fashion of the day. There
are four Chinese figures, a
pagoda with balustrade,
orange-trees in pots, and
boats. The backing fabric is
a cherry-coloured silk
damask of the mid-
eighteenth century (private
collection, Paris)

Page 85
Detail of the central motif

reign, had been associated with such excesses –
fiercely attacked by the caricaturists – that a
greater simplicity was the only development
possible.

In the 1770s therefore the lace industry was
already experiencing a sharp contraction of
demand. In Alençon for example a notable
person, Olivier de Saint-Vast, town magistrate,
became anxious about the situation. He wrote to
the director general of the manufacturers re-
porting that, to prevent the entire falling-off of
the production of Alençon and Argentan laces,
they must urge Queen Marie-Antoinette to
wear them at least once a week. On 18 September 1780, an anonymous official replied that he
had 'noticed that lace was, like other objects,
subject to the sway of fashion, and consequently
subject to revolutions . . . that the changes were a
misfortune for the makers and merchants,
whose work was diminishing; but that one could
not because of that restrict the taste of the
consumer, much less that of the Queen'. Would
that he had had no more than the revolutions of
fashion to concern him! The accounts of Mlle
Bertin and Mme Eloffe, fashion-suppliers to the
Queen, show nevertheless that she was still
ordering small amounts of lace in August 1792,
shortly before her arrest.

What remained of lace on the gowns at that
time was chiefly silk blonde, of which some was
made throughout Europe, but above all in
France, in Venice and in Spain. This lace is
made relatively quickly because its meshes, with
a central pinhole, are very large and its designs
extremely simple. Many children of both sexes
worked on it in orphanages or other charitable
institutions. Small boys as well as girls were
trained to make it from the age of five. Lace had
now lost its star role, and instead served mainly
to support other decorations. Threads of coloured chenille were carried across it, or artificial
flowers were threaded through its large meshes:
it had become a kind of tulle, bought by the
metre.

# The great laces of the eighteenth century and their characteristics

That the eighteenth century was a period of specialization was mentioned at the beginning of this chapter. Every lace centre, of whatever importance, produced a lace with well-defined technical characteristics. Also as already mentioned, a technique is easily exported, whereas a style may never be completely integrated elsewhere. When a particular lace was in fashion, it was of course copied everywhere, so that a place-name attached to a lace gives absolutely no guarantee of its provenance: Brussels might be made in France; Mechlin in Italy, Spain, Venice or Germany, etc. It is, however, generally considered that the very best quality pieces, in style as well as technique, could hardly have been produced except in the lace-centres where they originated. With this important qualification, it seems most suitable to describe one by one the laces in fashion in the eighteenth century under the place-names by which they are still known.

Lace chest. *c.* 1770
Private collection

The chest of drawers is of wood covered with red morocco. The drawers and the doors are padded with pale blue satin with darker blue braid. It contains a collection of antique laces – Venetian, Burano, Alençon, Brussels, Mechlin, blonde, etc.

Lappet (detail). Needle. 'Point de Sedan'. Alençon or Sedan, *c.* 1710
Linen 8 × 86 cm
Paris, private collection

# NEEDLE LACES

*Alençon*

The technical characteristics of Alençon lace are as follows: a *réseau* of looped meshes from about 1700; a cordonnet consisting of a core of thread covered with buttonhole stitches until about 1775, but sometimes made of horse-hair after that date; and decorative stitches called fillings (*modes*).

When fashions changed at the very beginning of the century, demanding laces ever lighter and more supple, the lacemakers of Alençon tried to adapt themselves to this development,

although still continuing to manufacture their classic point de France with its large hexagonal meshes until about 1740. In order to give more lightness and transparency to their laces, they had had the idea of introducing a réseau of simple meshes, not covered with buttonhole stitches. These meshes consisted little loops of thread which were linked both to each other and to a thread laid diagonally between the motifs. It seems established that this ground, so characteristic of Alençon, was already perfected in the latter part of the seventeenth century. Under the French regency (1715–23) luxuriant lace motifs, which appear also in the celebrated lace-patterned

silks of that time, invaded the ground, leaving little space for the réseau. This did not greatly matter, since the réseau was no more than a device to reduce the rigidity of needle lace. However, a little later, the aesthetic possibilities of this process were realized.

The motifs of Alençon lace of the first half of the seventeenth century were fairly similar to those of bobbin lace. They consisted at first of flowers and exotic fruits rendered in a great variety of decorative stitches. Then, during the reign of Louis XV, these motifs became more naturalistic. By naturalistic is not to be understood fidelity to nature, at least not yet. The designers of the period drew their

inspiration from nature, certainly, but lost no time in improving and redistributing its elements according to aesthetic criteria. Thus it was that their lace designs comprised flowers rendered with botanical precision – carnations, peonies, roses – but on a much larger scale than the vases in which they were placed; Chinese pagodas much smaller than the butterflies which fluttered around them, etc.

Before long, however, all these motifs dwindled, and the réseau took on more and more importance. From the 1740s it formed a wide clear ground against which small Rococo medallions in decorative stitches stood out well. Later, when these medallions

disappeared and their place was taken by delicate branches of cherry or flowering plum, the fine meshes of the réseau set these off without competing with them. Towards the end of the century, interest in the design of laces in general diminished to such an extent that from the 1780s the 'rivers' of fillings arranged along the edge of the lace provided almost its only ornamentation.

## Argentan

Argentan is distinguished from Alençon lace by the following technical characteristic: the réseau of Argentan is made of hexagonal meshes covered with buttonhole stitches, like the great

picoted meshwork of point de France from which it developed, but without the picots. It did not, like its neighbour Alençon adopt a lighter réseau at the end of the seventeenth century, but kept its large and heavy meshes until the middle of the eighteenth century. From the 1770s, the Argentan lacemakers found a means of lightening their meshes slightly simply by twisting a thread around them instead of covering them with buttonhole stitches. Unfortunately this produced a hazy effect which detracted from the appearance of the lace.

The designs of Argentan almost always contained a larger number of solid areas than did those of Alençon, and this was especially the case between 1730 and 1750. After that date, however, the two laces could hardly be distinguished in this respect, and only the technique of the réseaux justified the separate name. Almost certainly, the two types of lace were made without distinction in either town.

## Sedan

Point de Sedan has the same technical characteristics as Alençon, namely a ground of large picoted brides like those of point de France until about 1740 and, concurrently from the end of the seventeenth century, a réseau of looped meshes similar to those of Alençon. We have few detailed records of the making of lace in Sedan in the eighteenth century, but its reputation in that period was undoubtedly as high as it had been in the seventeenth century. Savary des Bruslons in his *Dictionnaire du commerce* notes that in 1759 in Sedan, 'laces gave work to several thousands of people'. 'Point de Sedan' generally designates a specific style rather than a particular technique. Its designs are composed of very ample motifs – vases full of huge flowers, vast fir-cones and pineapples – the scale was much larger than with any other lace. The diversity of decorative stitches is astonishing, and one can without exaggeration term the effect virtuoso. The arrangements are always teeming, and it is difficult to detect the mesh ground between the motifs. The contours of the motifs were not entirely raised by a cordonnet; this was placed only where it was likely to produce the best effect. An Oriental, particularly an Indo-Persian influence was strongly evident, and the motifs typical of Moghul India and Persia

appeared – trees of life, *botehs* and pomegranates. The texture of point de Sedan in general was much more supple than that of other needle laces. The thread was of great fineness, and sometimes slightly yellowish in colour.

It is probable that a number of 'Sedan' laces were made in Belgium, probably in Brussels, and in Alençon.

Some small pieces – notably lappets, engageantes and robings, as opposed to large flounces – were made as described above but without any raising. These were referred to as 'flat réseau Venise', or 'point d'Angleterre', or 'Brussels'. This is doubly confusing, firstly because it is likely that many of these 'réseau Venise' laces were made in the area of Brussels – including doubtless Sedan – rather than in Venice, and secondly because the name 'Angleterre', too, was used of Brussels and Flanders lace. A fuller study remains to be done on this controversial subject. 'Réseau Venise' is included here because it represents one of the most successful applications of the needle lace technique, as can be seen from the pieces illustrated.

# BOBBIN LACES

## Brussels

The technical characteristics of Brussels are as follows: it is a non-continuous-thread lace, with a ground of small hexagonal meshes, the two vertical sides of each mesh being made of four threads plaited four times – a type of ground known as 'droschel'; the motifs are worked in tight clothstitch with a massing of threads on their contours forming a shallow relief.

Brussels began to be appreciated during the last years of the seventeenth

century. Men adopted it to trim their long cravat of white batiste, one end of which was passed through a buttonhole of their coat to end in a rectangle of lace. As for women, they wore lace everywhere. Entire skirts were made of it, as were aprons, pleated flounces and, of course, bonnets and lappets. In furnishings, it was draped profusely in deep flounces around bathtubs or dressing-table mirrors.

The variety of designs of Brussels was enormous, for its technique allowed all sorts of fanciful arrangements. Nothing was too difficult for the Brussels lacemakers. They excelled at incorporating people, opulent flowers and luxuriant foliage, Chinese pagodas, dolphins sporting in the waves, boats with their crews, fountains and palm-trees. From 1685 to about 1750, neither the quality nor the quantity of these laces, of which numerous examples survive, ever lessened. The strength of the Brussels industry at that period lay both in its capacity to produce patterns in the French taste which then dominated Europe, and in its ability to adapt itself immediately to the slightest changes in fashion.

This said, Brussels was not exempt from the general insipidity which affected lace designs after 1760, although demand continued to be considerable.

## Bruges

The lace tradition of Bruges was probably no less old than that of other centres, but its productions developed no distinctive features until the nineteenth century. In the eighteenth century, the Brussels technique was used in Bruges, but with a softer thread, a looser clothstitch, more numerous

halfstitch areas, and more derivative designs. During this period, Bruges mainly specialized in trimmings for church vestments, especially albs and surplices.

## Binche

Binche is a lace of continuous-thread technique, in contrast to Brussels and Bruges. In other words, the work begins with a certain number of bobbins and generally finishes with the same number. All the threads used in Binche are of the same thickness – or rather, are of the same fineness, for it is a lace of gossamer lightness. Its solid areas are not of a uniform clothstitch; instead the motifs are worked with variable closeness, producing a characteristic shaded effect. Also attributable to the lacemakers of Binche was the discovery of the 'snowball' ground, which they used frequently and in large quantities. This *fond de neige* (not to be confused with the Venetian needle lace *point de neige*) resembles a crowd of spots or snowflakes. When the spots are larger they are called 'spiders'. This ground, though characteristic of Binche, is not exclusive to it, but appears also in Mechlin and Valenciennes laces. Before Valenciennes found its own style and technique, around 1740, it is sometimes difficult to distinguish it from Binche. The two producing towns are very close together. The solid areas of the lace became less uniform and less close in Binche than in Valenciennes.

## Valenciennes

In the eighteenth century Valenciennes was a continuous-thread lace, characterized by a very closely worked and uniform clothstitch. The meshes

Lappet (detail). Bobbins. 'Binche'. Binche, *c.* 1730
Linen
Calais, Musée des Beaux-Arts et de la Dentelle; inv. 86-1-10

Note the diversity of snowballs, and the solid design-areas alternately loosely and closely worked, a characteristic of Binche

Page 93
Cravat-end for a man (detail). Bobbins. 'Valenciennes'. Valenciennes or Binche, 1700-25
Linen 30 × 35 cm
Lyons, Musée Historique des Tissus; inv. 28874-I.4466

This cravat-end, like all continuous-thread laces, is made of several bands joined together: here there are seven. It is not possible otherwise to produce large pieces by this technique

of its réseau were plaited on all sides. They were at first round, but became very square about 1740. It was not until that year that French bobbin laces acquired a reputation comparable to that of French needle laces, and that they did so was due entirely to Valenciennes. The lacemakers of that town succeeded in freeing themselves of all Flemish influence, producing a lace of a style which still called to mind, long after it had ceased to be made at Valenciennes, a feminine image, somewhere between the chaste and the coquettish, which rightly or wrongly all the world associates with France and the French. The hard clarity of the ground, the firmness of the outlines, the creamy whiteness of the solid areas of design are the features which distinguish Valenciennes from other laces.

Indeed its whiteness was so renowned at the time that it was claimed it could not be obtained outside the walls of the town. References to 'vraie Valenciennes' (true Valenciennes) often appear in the inventories and accounts of the 1760s, as distinct, it would seem, from the imitations made in neighbouring villages. Valenciennes, like most of the bobbin laces, was worn in the summer, while needle laces were worn in winter.

## Mechlin

Mechlin is a continuous-thread lace, originating in the town of that name which is situated to the north-west of Brussels, between Antwerp and Bruges. It is characterized by the use of a thicker thread encircling the motifs, and by a réseau of meshes with four

threads plaited on the two sides parallel to the footing. The decoration nearly always includes a trefoil or quatrefoil motif, which also appears in the coat of arms of the town. It seems that the town of Mechlin (Malines) succeeded during nearly the whole of the eighteenth century in retaining the monopoly of manufacture of the most beautiful of these laces, although several attempts were made in France, notably at Villiers-le-Bel to the north of Paris, to establish its production. Although at first it was much sought after for its incomparable lightness, and for the quality of its designs, the contours of which were emphasized by a thicker thread which encircled them, Mechlin suffered the same fate as all the other laces at the end of the century. Production in the town almost ceased, not to resume again until the nineteenth century, and then in other places.

## Lille

Lille is a continuous-thread bobbin lace with its motifs encircled by a thicker thread, as in Mechlin. However the réseau of Lille is different. It is called *fond clair* because its meshes are made of two threads only, simply crossed over. Large-scale manufacture of the lace appears to have begun in the eighteenth century, perhaps towards 1750, though its origins date back to the end of the sixteenth century. Its technique is simple and its motifs are frugal, so that it can be made quickly. It was produced in a number of towns around Lille, particularly Arras. It was also made in many other parts of France and elsewhere, for example at Tønder in Denmark and at the convent of Waldstena in Sweden. An English

Furnishing flounce.
Bobbins. 'Mechlin'.
Mechlin *c.* 1700
Linen 30 × 90 cm
Paris, private collection

The large scale of the motifs is unusual for a bobbin lace. This pattern appears to be adapted from a design for a furnishing fabric of the period, and is the only piece of Mechlin of such size known to the author. Mechlin, being a continuous-thread lace, can only be made in narrow pieces. Here the flounce is made by the joining together of strips about 20 cm in width, for the production of which some 2,000 bobbins would be required. The manufacture of deep flounces by the non-continuous-thread technique is much easier and more logical, so it is not surprising that efforts of this kind were not usual

variety, made in the Midlands, was
called Bucks point.

### Blonde

This is a continuous-thread bobbin
lace with a very characteristic réseau of
meshes with a central pinhole. It is
named after the cream silk thread
which is generally used, but blonde is
also made in black or coloured silk, or
in metal thread. Although silk laces
were made from the seventeenth century, notably in the region to the north
of Paris, the term blonde was not well
established until the 1760s. Blonde was
not an expensive lace except when
worked with real gold or silver threads.
Its very simple motifs, often of trefoils
or quatrefoils, were surrounded with a
thicker thread, which might be silk of a
different colour, or a velvety or curly
chenille. Ribbons or sprays of artificial
flowers were threaded through the
holes of the large meshes. Because
blonde was easily and quickly worked,
a large quantity was produced in religious and charitable institutions. The
towns of Caen and Rouen made it a
speciality. In Venice, a lot of blonde
lace of black silk was used for the *baute*,
a little cape attached to the hat and
falling to the elbows, worn by both
men and women. Spain consumed
large quantities of blonde for mantil-
las, the popularity of which began in
the eighteenth century. The floss or
coloured silks used to make these
laces were not durable, so that very
few examples of eighteenth-century
blondes remain, despite the enormous
quantities produced.

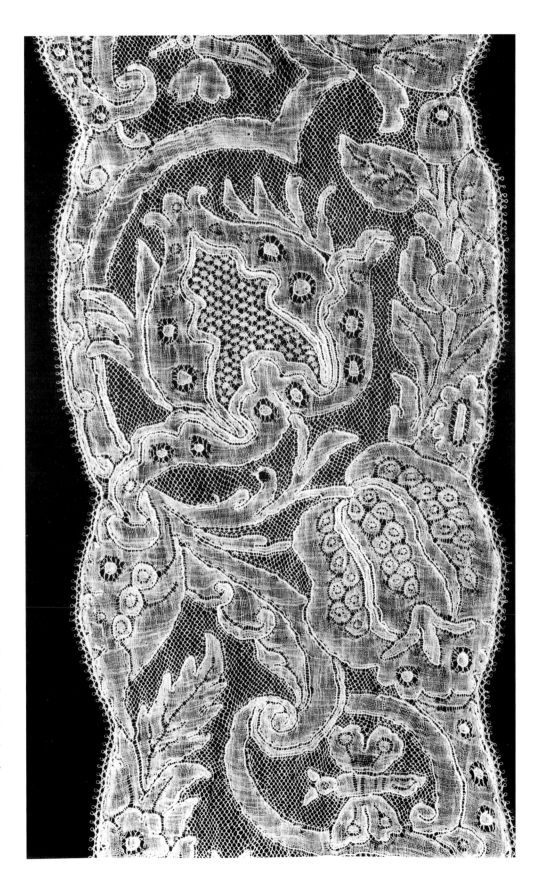

Opposite:
Flounce (detail). Bobbins.
'Brussels, called point
d'Angleterre'. Brussels,
c. 1730
Linen 64 × 300 cm
Paris, Musée des Arts
Décoratifs; inv. 55851
Formerly collection of the
Prince and Princess de la
Tour d'Auvergne-Lauraguais

Below:
Alb flounce (detail).
Bobbins. 'Brussels, called
point d'Angleterre'.
Brussels, c. 1755
Linen 60 × 320 cm
Italy, private collection

The central palm-tree,
symbol of paradise,
suggests that this flounce
was intended for a church
vestment. The large picotéd
bars of the ground are
generally an indication of
Bruges manufacture

Following pages:
Cravat-end for a man.
Bobbins. 'Brussels, called
point d'Angleterre'.
Brussels, c. 1715
Linen 35 × 25 cm
From *Musée d'art et
d'histoire de la Ville de
Genève, Dentelles anciennes*,
Paris, n.d.

Hunting scenes with figures
dressed in fantastic
costumes, and small
squirrels nibbling nuts next
to a man blowing a horn

Flounce (detail). Needle.
'Réseau Venise'.
Venice/Burano, *c.* 1760
Linen 16 × 132 cm
Paris, private collection

The working of such a
piece, perfectly executed in
very fine thread, demands
enormous skill. The
decorative stitches so
perfectly placed confer a
great elegance on the
design, which appears to
show a Japanese influence.
The form of the meshes is
typical of Venice/Burano.

Flounce (detail).
Needle. 'Argentan'.
Alençon/Argentan,
*c.* 1750
Linen 64 × 320 cm
Amsterdam,
Rijksmuseum; inv.
R.B.K. 16004

The decoration in
*chinoiserie* style
appears to be
influenced by that
of the tapestry
*L'Audience de
l'empereur de Chine*,
several examples of
which were
manufactured at
Beauvais between
1725 and 1745, and
which were very
popular

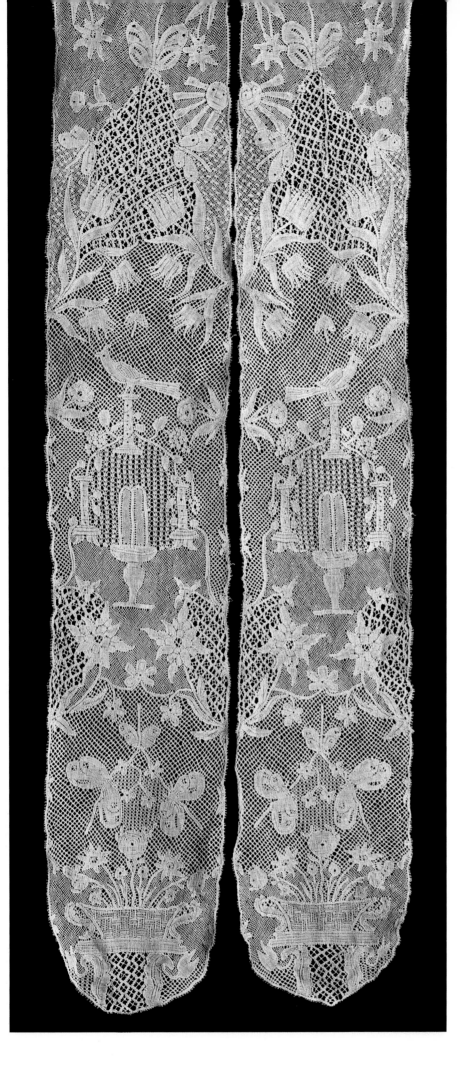

Pair of lappets (detail).
Bobbins. 'Flanders'.
Flanders, the area of
Mechlin or Antwerp,
*c.* 1760
Linen 9 × 118 cm (each)
Italy, private collection

This piece is unique, both
for the naive character of
its decoration – with suns,
birds, fountains and
butterflies – and for its
technique. The ground of
decorative stitches is the
only one of its kind known
to the author

Flounce (detail). Needle.
'Argentan'. Argentan or
Bayeux, *c.* 1855
Linen 61 × 315
Paris, Musée des Arts
Décoratifs; inv. 52848.
Formerly collection of the
Prince and Princess de la
Tour d'Auvergne-
Lauraguais

The technique of shaded
flowers, where the solid
areas are composed of
stitches more or less tightly
packed, dates only from
1855 (see the chapter
dealing with the nineteenth
century). The decoration of
this piece borrows almost
all its elements from the
style of Louis XVI, but has
not been able to recreate
the simple elegance of that
period. Moreover, in the
reign of Louis XVI large
flounces were no longer
fashionable. This piece was
certainly intended for an
exhibition. It was probably
made in one of the great
French workshops of the
nineteenth century, such as
that of Lefébure at Bayeux

Alb flounce (detail).
Bobbins. 'Brussels'.
Brussels, *c.* 1804
Linen 64 × 300 cm
Paris, Musée des Arts
Décoratifs; inv. 11094 A

The bobbin-made motifs
are appliquéd on to a
droschel ground. This
flounce trimmed the alb of
Cardinal Fesch, uncle of
Napoleon I and Archbishop
of Lyons. He would have
worn it at the time of the
coronation of the Emperor
in 1804. The design,
composed of flowers called
'imperial crown', is perhaps
an allusion to this event.
Several copies of this alb
flounce were made.
The Rijksmuseum of
Amsterdam, for example,
has one where the motifs
are applied to a machine
net

Woven fabric
Convolvulus and lace edgings. Composition by Bérard, paper plan by Arpin
Silk velvet; on a ground of silk taffeta
Commissioned through the Maison Bonnet frère of Lille for Her Majesty, Queen Victoria
Lyons, Bérard et Poncet, 1861
67 × 92 cm
Lyons, Musée Historique des Tissus; inv. 21805.872.XIX.1

The lace represented is of point de gaze type. It has hexagonal
meshes with picots and a border of large marguerites

# THE NINETEENTH
# CENTURY

# VIRTUOSITY AND
# MECHANICS

Shawl
Needle. 'Point de gaze'. Brussels, *c.* 1890
Linen 130 × 300 cm
Florence, Palazzo Davanzati; inv. Stoffe 1366; cat. no. 68

The shawl is worn over an afternoon gown of Parma silk taffeta
embroidered with yellow straw
Florence, Galleria del Costume di Palazzo Pitti; inv. T.A.3076.9
Acquisition fund of Salvatore Ferragamo; cat. no. 16

(863)

Even before the great political upheaval of the French Revolution, laces were no longer in fashion. Certainly they still existed, but they were no longer spoken of. They were now used to trim undergarments – petticoats, drawers, camisoles – and as these laces were not seen, it was logical to devote less care to their creation. Soon, all the centres where the industry managed to survive set themselves to produce similar laces, either by needle or by bobbins, in narrow widths and with dull and repetitive designs.

The situation was the same in Flanders and in Italy, in France and in Spain. In France, the revolutionary authorities realized nevertheless that lace furnished work for a large number of people, especially in Normandy. While decrying the 'expensive and frivolous' products of this industry, the Minister of the Interior Saint-Just, responsible for trade, in February 1794 (year III) granted a subsidy to the town council of Alençon in an attempt to encourage the resumption of manufacture. France needed exports, and besides, claimed the official report drawn up for the occasion: 'it is impossible that the lacemakers could so quickly have forgotten the skills which made their manufacture famous'. But the best clients of the Alençon lacemakers had gone, and even if revolutionary France managed to export laces, for example to America, the quantities were likely to be small.

When Napoleon I arrived on the scene, therefore, a core of knowledgeable lacemakers still existed, and he lost no time in putting them to work. Like Colbert long before him, Napoleon wanted to encourage the luxury industries, not just for commercial reasons but for considerations of national prestige. The new Imperial protocol required the wearing of lace, by men as well as by women. For his coronation, Napoleon himself wore a jabot of Alençon, 'superfine, with wolf's teeth' (that is, with a sharply dentate edge), ordered from the firm of Beuvry and Company. It is to be seen in the well-known painting of the Coronation by Jacques-Louis

Formal court gown of the
Empress Marie-Louise (?).
Bobbins. 'Blonde'. France,
*c.* 1810
White chenilled silk
decorated with threads of
silver
Paris, Musée de la Mode et
du Costume de la Ville de
Paris; inv. 10640

This gown may have
belonged to the Empress
Marie-Louise. A formal
outfit in blonde, chenille
and silver, delivered to the
Empress by the supplier
M. Leroy on the 5 April
1810, was part of the
trousseau presented by
Napoleon I to his wife.
The design of the dress is
not specified, however, and
we cannot be sure that this
is the same dress

Page 110
Parisian costume. Print.
Court gown, 1808
Paris, Bibliothèque
Nationale

Note the similarity between
the gown shown here and
that in the photograph
opposite

David, which now hangs in the palace of Versailles. Men, however, no longer wore lace except when compelled to do so. Woollen cloth and exclusively sombre colours had replaced the multi-coloured silks and velvets, gold and silver thread and floral embroidery of the eighteenth century. The role of men in the nineteenth century was to serve as a foil for women, not to rival them. Lace disappeared, perhaps for ever, from masculine clothes.

On the other hand, the trousseau of the Emperor's second wife, Marie-Louise of Austria, included a large number of laces of all kinds, though with much more Angleterre – that is to say, Brussels – than Alençon, for the lace industry of south Flanders now also had to be subsidized since it had become part of the Empire. She possessed a dozen shawls or veils in Angleterre, as well as three gowns entirely 'in designs of leaves, roses and spots', or again, 'with open festoons, rose-buds, a scattering of leaves, dots, stars, poppies and tulips', amounting in all to about 70,000 francs in the currency of the time, out of the 80,000 francs which Napoleon had allocated to her. By comparison, the only object in Alençon which figures on the list, a shawl supplied by a Monsieur Lenormand who was also a merchant of cashmeres, cost only 3,200 francs. If prestige laces survived, it was therefore in large part thanks to the Imperial orders. The laces of this period were often ornamented with motifs of bees, hives, crowns, laurel-wreaths and Roman fasces, all symbols adopted by the First Empire.

As for blonde, it did relatively well since it was much less costly and, above all, it was now more and more in fashion. However, it resembled less and less a true lace, becoming increasingly like a tulle of which only the borders were decorated with motifs. The technique used to make it had also changed. Its network of meshes was now the same as that of Lille, made with two threads merely twisted. As early as 1803, an exhibition of blonde lace was organized at Caen. At the next exhibition, which took place there in

Parisian costume. Print.
Bridal outfit, *c.* 1823
Paris, Bibliothèque
Nationale

The title indicates that the
wedding veil is of
'Angleterre', in other
words, of Brussels bobbin
lace

Page 112
Gown. Bobbins. 'Blonde'.
France, Caen or Rouen,
*c.* 1820
Cream silk
Paris, Musée de la Mode et
du Costume de la Ville de
Paris; inv. 17534

Coif known as *Sonnekapp*
or *Pfanerad* (sunbonnet, or
peacock's tail). France, Bas-
Rhin, Meistratzheim,
1800–60
Paris, Musée des Arts et
Traditions Populaires; inv.
40.26.15

Bonnet embroidered with
gold thread and spangles;
edging of gold bobbin lace
possibly taken from an
eighteenth-century habit.
The pleated machine lace
surrounding the bonnet, and
mounted on a supporting
frame, would have been
added about 1860

1806, a manufacturer, a Monsieur Louis Horel,
showed a large shawl which had taken three
lacemakers three months to make, and for which
it had been necessary to use, he said, 3,000
bobbins and 18,000 pins. Blonde, especially in
black silk, was also made in and around Chantilly, to the north of Paris. But this traditional
centre for silk lace, crushed by the competition
from Normandy, practically ceased activity in
the 1840s.

The prosperity which the lace exhibitions
appeared to indicate was of short duration. It
was curbed, even before the downfall of the

Emperor in 1812, by the appearance of machine
net. The technology of the manufacture of
machine net, based on the principle of the
stocking machines already developed in the
eighteenth century, was perfected by the Eng-
lishman Heathcoat at the turn of the century
and patented in 1809. Three years later, in 1812,
a Monsieur de Rens, president of the association
of French lace manufacturers, wrote to the
Imperial authorities asking them to prohibit the
wearing of machine net, both for everyday
clothes and for court dress. One can understand
M. de Rens' concern, for in 1810 the Empress
Marie-Louise owned no fewer than eighteen
gowns of net, embroidered in white, blue, pink,
gold and silver. The engravings of the period
indicate that the lace effect, if not lace itself, was
much more in fashion than is commonly
supposed.

Concurrently with this fashion, another
phenomenon was developing during the first
years of the century. Regional costumes, and
most particularly the head-dresses, were diver-
sifying. The reasons for this development are
extremely complex, and it is not possible to
detail them here. It may simply be stated that
under the *Ancien Régime*, some regional differ-
ences of dress had certainly existed, but in
general peasant dress was no more than a
modest version of urban costume. In the
nineteenth century on the other hand, the
difference between town and country clothing
was exaggerated. Every region, every provincial
or market town, developed a costume different
from that of its neighbour. The peasant head-
dresses which up to then had often been simple
white bonnets grew at times to gigantic proportions, notably in Normandy and Brittany, and
in the Low Countries. Elaborate constructions
had to be held in shape by means of a
framework, and all were ornamented with a
profusion of lace, or in some instances, were
entirely made of it. This provided new outlets
for the lace industry, especially, of course, for its
most humble productions. Quality did not

Coif known as *capot* or *grand bonnet*. France, Saintonge, 1830–60
Paris, Musée des Arts et Traditions Populaires; inv. 987.5.1

The shape of this head-dress was developed at the beginning of the century.

The machine Mechlin, arranged in pipe-like folds, was probably contemporary. The embroidered machine net, on the other hand, is a later addition, *c.* 1860. It looks as though it has been reassembled

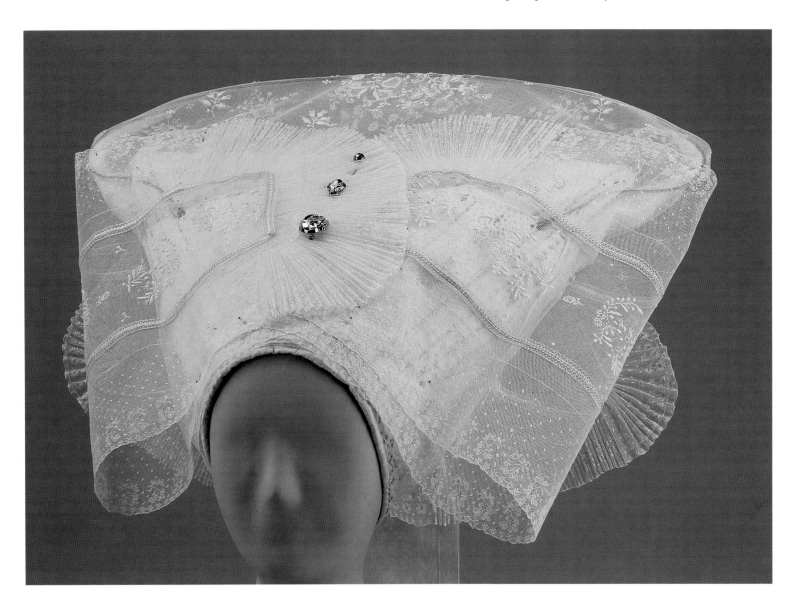

matter so much as quantity in these head-dresses, where in any case the lace was frequently folded into tight little pleats which made it difficult to distinguish the motifs.

However, by a reciprocal effect not unusual in fashion, peasant laces in due course influenced the dress of the elegant women of the middle classes. The 1830s witnessed an important revival of lace, despite serious competition from white embroidery. This affected only bobbin laces, however, and needle laces remained confined to their role as an aristocratic and slightly outmoded finery.

The development of machine net had given rise to a new form of lace industry: appliqué work. Bobbin or needle lace motifs were formed separately and then applied to a ground of machine net. In the best pieces, the net was then cut away behind the motifs to give an openness similar to that of real lace. The plaited mesh ground of laces such as Brussels and Mechlin took a long time to make, and it is easy to see what a saving of time appliqué represented. Of course the value of the product was reduced: since its execution was more rapid, it was less expensive to buy. This served in turn to

*Marie-Caroline de Bourbon-Salerne, Duchesse d'Aumale, in 1830*, François-Xavier Winterhalter, 1842
Oil on canvas
Versailles, Musée National de Château et des Trianons

The Duchess wears a complete outfit of silk blonde. The design of her stole is inspired by that of cashmere shawls, while that of her flounce is composed of flowering sprigs typical of the 1840s when the painting was done. Note that contrary to the practice in the eighteenth century, the flounces are stitched to the gown without a heading to hide the seams

Scarf or wedding veil (detail). Bobbins. 'Blonde'. France, probably Bayeux, *c.* 1835
Linen, 41 × 40 cm (?)
Hartford, Connecticut, Wadsworth Atheneum; inv. 715. Gift of Mrs James B. Cone

This blonde, of a design inspired by the cashmere shawls of the 1800s, is in very fine linen, rather than silk, which indicates a Bayeux production

Flounce for a crinoline (detail). Bobbins. 'Chantilly'. France, Bayeux, *c.* 1855
Black silk, 60 × 1400 cm
Paris, private collection

This flounce, 14 metres long, was intended to trim a crinoline. Like all Chantilly laces of this size, it is made of horizontal bands about 12 cm wide joined together by an invisible point de raccroc, made with a needle. The quality of the workmanship, as well as the lightly silvered effect of the thread, are distinguishing marks of a Bayeux production

stimulate the production of real laces. The great prosperity which the industrial age had brought to the European bourgeoisie benefitted all luxury industries. Work done by hand was valued for its own sake, and accordingly it was natural that machines should begin to imitate hand-made products, particularly lace, in a convincing manner. Little by little, lace decoration regained its importance, in keeping with the deeper and deeper flounces now ornamenting gowns.

Initially, during the decade 1825–35, laces drew their inspiration from the designs of cashmere shawls, which had been very much in vogue since the end of the eighteenth century. Particularly on the blondes, one sees the motifs of curving palms, *botehs* full of tiny flowers, and rows of Persian carnations. Interestingly, these patterns were no longer in fashion on the cashmere shawls themselves, where the decoration had by then become more crowded. Such a time-lag is common in the applied arts, when it is gradually realized that certain motifs can be adapted to other crafts.

Weddings were now a prime occasion for wearing laces. The white gown and veil were a relatively recent introduction, appearing towards the end of the eighteenth century, and not really *de rigueur* until the 1830s. The gowns were often of embroidered net, or of white lawn trimmed with Mechlin, blonde or Brussels; the veil, in the form of a long rectangle, was worn caught at its mid-point to the top of the chignon, so that the long ends fell gracefully over the back of the gown.

Valenciennes, meanwhile, had become the supreme lace of intimate apparel. All the personal linen of girls and young women was trimmed with it; and it also formed the wide edgings of embroidered handkerchiefs. It was now worked in a more rapid manner which will be described later. It was scarcely produced any longer in the town of Valenciennes, although small neighbouring towns such as Bailleul still made it. Ypres and Ghent now specialized in the manufacture of Valenciennes of such high quality that the lace was spoken of as 'Valenciennes de Brabant', the name of the Belgian province in which these two towns are situated.

The nineteenth century saw a perfect mania for industrial exhibitions. Not a year passed without such an exhibition being organized in

*Louise d'Orléans, Queen of Belgium*, François-Xavier Winterhalter, *c.* 1846 Versailles, Musée National du Château et des Trianons

The Queen wears a gown trimmed with two deep flounces of black Chantilly

Fashion plate, c. 1865
Paris, Bibliothèque des Arts
Décoratifs, collection
Maciet

Shawl of black Chantilly
lace with a decoration of
naturalistic flowers
bordered with motifs
resembling railway tracks

one or other European country. The new lace patterns were well displayed next to antique laces, which, it was beginning to be realized, offered an incomparable source of stylistic inspiration. Soon lace manufacturers were happily blending elements of the styles of Louis XIV, Louis XV and Louis XVI, all in the same lace-design. By 1839 the house of Violard, manufacturer of silk blondes and Indian cashmeres in Paris and at Caen, was showing at the Paris Exhibition examples of black laces with decorations of pyramidal bouquets and cartouches in seventeenth-century style. In his report on the exhibition the editor of the *Journal des demoiselles* took no account of M. Violard, even though he had received a bronze medal, but on the contrary congratulated the manufacturers of the Mirecourt and Le Puy areas, commenting that they were now offering designs so charming that 'it is no longer necessary for us to get our laces by stripping them from religious statues in country churches'. These two regions were enjoying a renewal of lace-production. At Mirecourt, laces were being made in imitation of those of Brussels and Bruges, especially Duchesse, and appliqué, as well as a furnishing guipure partly made with a braid of thick silk. The latter was called 'guipure arabe', for it was inspired by the corded embroideries of the North African countries which France was just beginning to colonize. In his report on the International Exhibition of 1867 Félix Aubry, a celebrated lace manufacturer of the Le Puy region, described with an honesty which did him credit the rival production of Mirecourt as representing 'the most fertile [imagination] . . . an unflagging avant-garde which stimulates innovation, points the road to follow, and gives rivals a beneficial and energetic impulse'.

Despite these generous expressions of enthusiasm, it was the laces of Le Puy that would be remembered in history, not those of Mirecourt. In terms of the numbers of workers, Le Puy was probably the most important French centre for bobbin lace at the time. In that same year, 1867, it was estimated that more than 100,000 young girls and women of the region were occupied in the work. They made all kinds of laces: Torchon, a slightly dense lace with shell motifs; Chantilly of a quality inferior to that of Normandy; metal laces; a heavy guipure of black silk with designs in 'gothic' style, much used by

widows; and above all Cluny, a lace said to be derived from sixteenth-century patterns shown at the Musée de Cluny, Paris.

If the lacemakers of Le Puy were more numerous, those of Normandy supplied a more sophisticated clientèle with considerable financial means. This clientèle was to expand again under the Second Empire, in the course of which France, like England at the time, enjoyed a period of unprecedented prosperity, due partly to colonization and the world-wide expansion of trade which resulted. The enormous crinolines in fashion during the years 1850 to 1870 were an ideal support for the display of lace-designs, now of unparalleled richness. The wife of Napoleon III, the Empress Eugénie de Montijo, was young and beautiful and loved lace. She loved black laces, like those of her native Spain, and the laces of Alençon and Argentan which Marie-Antoinette had worn, for she worshipped the Queen's memory. As it happened, the manufacture of both these types of lace, the black bobbin Chantilly and the needle-made Alençon/Argentan, was in the hands of a dynamic French entrepreneur, August Lefébure.

Lefébure was a man of modern times, for he understood that division of labour was the key to achieving production sufficiently intensive to meet the demand, and sufficiently flexible to respond rapidly to changes of fashion. The young workers whom he trained in his workshops in Alençon and Bayeux – where a strict discipline reigned – were very specialized. Some made only the solid areas of design, others only the decorative fillings or raised outlines, others again the réseau. Even though a certain amount of specialization had probably already been known in the seventeenth and eighteenth centuries, for example in the Royal manufacturies, it had never been so systematized. Lefébure's policy was crowned with commercial success; but the very perfection of work required of the lacemakers resulted in a total uniformity and regularity which paradoxically ended by making the laces of these workshops appear mechanical. The sumptuous patterns then in fashion for laces were conceived to display the technical prowess involved in their production, and for the time being this distinguished them from machine laces. However, the bouquets of cabbage roses, lilacs, and hydrangeas, iris and convolvulus, so admirably

rendered in black silk Chantilly, the beribboned baskets, the flowery wreaths, the doves of Marie-Antoinette style Alençon – these the constantly improving lace machines would soon be able to copy in a convincing manner. Machine bobbin-laces in particular would be so well produced that it would be difficult to distinguish them with the naked eye from hand-made laces.

For the moment, however, the demand for lace was so strong that there was room for both the real and the false. France set the fashion, but her production was not large enough to supply the world market. Belgium, where Alençon and Venise were now made in workshops – some of which belonged to big French merchants – produced very large quantities of Valenciennes, point de gaze, Brussels appliqué, and a new sort of bobbin lace known as Duchesse. Duchesse was inspired by Brussels patterns of the seventeenth century. It possessed a very individual

style, immediately recognizable. There was no réseau of meshes; its motifs of strongly ribbed leaves and five-petalled flowers were linked by plaited brides. A great deal of this lace was worked in the Bruges area, but it was also made in the large workshops of Brussels. There, it was often incrusted with medallions of needle-made point de gaze, which had become a great Brussels speciality, and was to some extent an imitation of Alençon, though its light mesh ground differed from that of Alençon. It was a very highly priced lace, in which the rich – some would say *nouveau riche* – decorations were only equalled by those of Chantilly. The somewhat excessive virtuosities of its effects contrasted with the sobriety of taste which continued to characterize Alençon. But the elegant astringency of Alençon was no longer suited Second Empire society, which encouraged people to flaunt their wealth. Point de gaze therefore little by little gained ascendancy over the other

Edging. Bobbins. 'Chantilly'. France, Le Puy-en-Velay, 1835–45 Black silk

The design represents the well-known fable of La Fontaine, *The Fox and the Raven*

Page 122
Afternoon gown trimmed with black Chantilly, *c.* 1855
Bronze-coloured watered silk, bobbin-made Chantilly in black silk
Paris, Union Française des Arts du Costume; inv. 61–25–2

The Chantilly lace was probably made in the region of Le Puy, rather than in Normandy

Parasol with ivory handle.
Bobbins. 'Chantilly'.
**France, Bayeux, *c*. 1865**
Black silk, diameter 70 cm
Italy, private collection

Page 125
Shawl (detail). Machine
Chantilly. France, Calais,
*c*. 1880
Black silk 130 × 300 cm
Florence, Palazzo
Davanzati

The design, with its large
Medici vase and flower-
shaped ornaments, was
inspired by that of the
furnishing silks and point
de France of the Louis
XIV period. The machine
net and the knitted
technique of the motifs,
replacing the characteristic
halfstitch of hand-made
Chantilly, can be clearly
seen.
The shawl is displayed over
an evening gown of taffeta,
satin and mauve silk
organza with the label
'Madame Grazini, 47
Strada Cavallenizza a
Chiapa [Naples]', of *c*.
1878. Florence, Galleria del
Costume di Palazzo Pitti;
inv. dep. 439; cat. no. 78

Border of a mourning
handkerchief. Bobbins.
'Chantilly'. France, Bayeux
*c*. 1885
Black silk 35 × 34 cm
Lyons, Musée Historique
des Tissus; inv. 32065

The decoration of iris and
ferns was often used by the
lace house Georges
Martin/Compagnie des
Indes. The high quality of
its manufacture points to
the same source

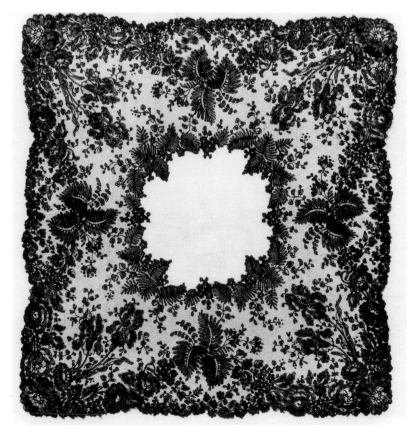

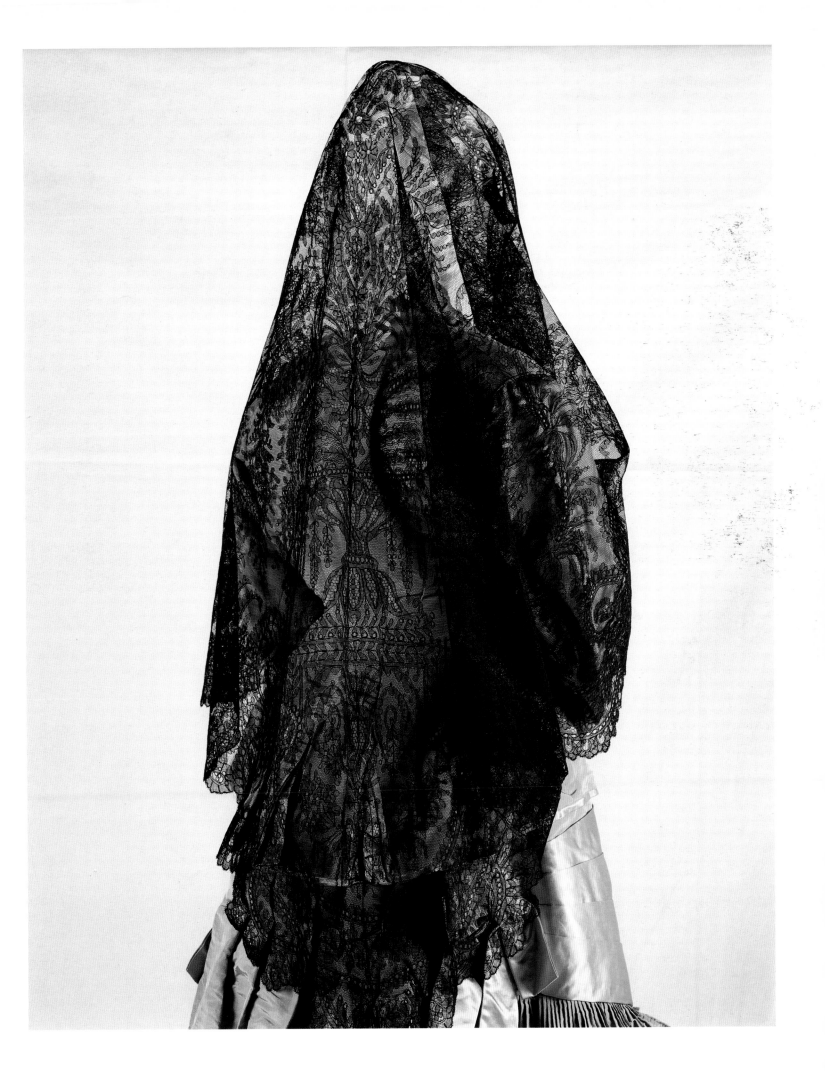

Shawl of pink silk (detail).
Bobbins and needle,
'nineteenth-century point
d'Angleterre'. Brussels,
c. 1890
Linen 21 × 3 cm
Italy, private collection

The solid areas of the
design are bobbin-made,
while the decorative
stitches and the ground are
worked with the needle.
This combination of the
two techniques was called
'point d'Angleterre' by the
Belgian manufacturers who
made it fashionable at the
end of the last century,
thereby increasing the
general confusion
surrounding the term

needle laces, and even the Normandy
lacemakers began to make it.

Belgium and France exported a large part of
their production, especially to North America,
where no true hand-made lace industry existed,
and to South America where a great deal of lace
was traditionally worn.

As for Italy, the manufacture of lace there
had revived again on a large scale. The peasant
costumes of the different regions had evolved as
in other countries, though lace was used not so
much for women's head-dresses – which indeed
scarcely existed in Italy, since the peasants wore
hats or pieces of cloth on their heads – as for the
chemise and, above all, the apron. But there was
another important element in the renewal of
prosperity for Italian lace: the souvenir industry. The nineteenth century was the age of
cultural pilgrimages for educated persons, and
of travel for others. Italy, like Greece, possessed

two great attractions: culture and exoticism. Its
wealth of monuments – classical, Renaissance
and Baroque – made it the cultural tour *par
excellence*, while the variety of its costumes and
dialects, the physical and cultural isolation of
some of its regions, and its social and economic
structures untouched by industrialization,
made it a favourite resort for the curious. The
cheap labour which was plentiful in Italy
provided 'souvenirs' for these travellers, and
lace in particular sold very well. The Italian
lacemakers had a long tradition behind them
and they were talented, but they were not
organized as were their French or Belgian
counterparts. They knew how to make everything, so they made everything; in particular
copies of Renaissance patterns with which they
had never lost their affinity, but equally, adaptations, on the whole mediocre, of fashionable
laces. All the Ligurian coastal region, for

example, made bobbin laces in the style of ancient Genoese passements, with Cluny and Torchon in addition. The lacemakers of Abruzzi made copies of Mechlin, as well as peasant laces of a non-distinctive style. Venice and its region of course made needle laces, but especially copies of cutwork, reticella and other punto in aria after the Renaissance pattern-books which a Venetian publisher, Oncagna, had issued in facsimile, as well as bobbin laces, in particular at Pallestrina. This production singularly complicates the task of present-day historians, for it is difficult to distinguish the laces of the years 1830 to 1900 from pieces made some two and a half centuries earlier.

The little town of Chioggia, near Venice, which had specialized in bobbin lace, now produced quantities of embroidered filet, called Venetian filet.

From the north to the south, the whole of Italy made lace, but this production, extensive as it was, was badly organized and inefficient commercially. Above all, its approach to style was traditional, and this denied it the important outlets created by fashion. Italy therefore never for a moment offered serious competition to the lace industries of France and Belgium.

In France, the fall of the Second Empire in 1870, after a disastrous war against Germany, was followed by a period of economic and social unrest which struck a serious blow at luxury industries such as lace, not only in France itself but in all the neighbouring countries. A generation later, in the last years of the century, the lace industry had become synonymous with machine lace, while hand-made lace had become an 'art'.

Fan with sticks and guards of pierced mother-of-pearl. Leaf of needle-made 'point de gaze'. Brussels, c. 1885 Linen
Collection Maryse Volet

The design is of a tiger and a lion roaring amidst palm-trees. The lion holds a parrot beneath its paw. In contrast, the border is very classical, with interlacings and marguerites. The workmanship is of excellent quality. The leaf was probably produced by one of the celebrated Belgian houses, perhaps for a colonial exhibition

# The great laces of the nineteenth century and their characteristics

*The series of nineteenth-century names apparently repeats those of the preceding century: however certain laces kept the same names but changed their characters, or their techniques, or their places of manufacture.*

## NEEDLE LACES

### Alençon

The technique of Alençon remained fundamentally as it had been in the eighteenth century: it consisted a ré-seau of looped meshes, a thin cordonnet, varied fillings – with, however, an important innovation dating from 1855: shaded motifs. These were made by means of a series of stitches more or less closely packed inside a particular part of a motif – a rose-petal for example – to obtain a very realistic effect of light and shade.

The manufacture of Alençon was resumed on a grand scale from the 1830s by French merchants such as Videcoq and Simon, the house of Verdé-Delisle, the Compagnie des Indes (also merchants of cashmere shawls), and above all Lefébure. One of the distinctive marks of the Lefébure workshops was the horse-hair passed through the picots of the motifs and the border in order to stiffen them. The laces of these great firms were nearly always of linen thread, but they had begun to introduce cotton for lace manufacture. Cotton thread is cheaper and more elastic than linen, but also more brittle and much fluffier. Its use aroused enthusiasm in some and opprobrium in others.

Fashion plate, *c.* 1865
Paris, Bibliothèque des Arts Décoratifs; collection Maciet

The immense shawl, worn folded in two, with a false hood decorated with Eastern-style tassels, appears to be of point de gaze or application d'Angleterre. These exceptionally large pieces were usually made by machine at this time

Above:
Flounce (detail).
Needle. 'Alençon'.
France, Alençon, *c.* 1810
Linen 10 × 95 cm
Italy, private
collection

Below:
Flounce. Needle.
'Alençon'. Italy,
Burano, *c.* 1880
Cotton 10 × 240 cm
Italy, private
collection

Note the difference in execution between the two flounces. In the flounce above, the lace is light and transparent, the meshes of the ground are sharp, the design is clear and the cordonnet taut. The very pointed scallops along the edge are known as 'wolf's teeth'. They are characteristic of the period 1800 to 1815. In the flounce below, the mesh ground is cloudy, as if streaky, and the design of little flowers aligned in the manner of the 1830s assorts badly with the milky aspect of the ground. It is almost certainly an imitation of Alençon made in Burano. Copies of Alençon in First Empire style, and of the years 1830 to 1850, were common at the end of the nineteenth century: Lefébure in particular made many of them. One can only distinguish these imitations from the earlier originals by the thread, which is always more yellowish in the copies, and by the stiffer and more crowded method of working. Also, the copies always included horsehair in the picots of the cordonnets and of the free edges

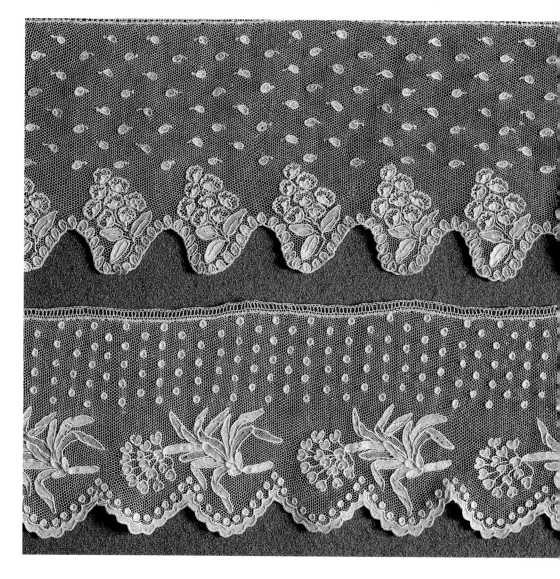

Certainly cotton does not possess that slightly shiny patina which characterizes linen.

The poverty of designs at the end of the eighteenth century and the beginning of the nineteenth was followed, in the course of the Second Empire, by a perhaps excessive richness. Motifs were still inspired by the style of the reign of Louis XVI, but had neither its graceful proportions nor its restraint. They were thrown in profusion over the lace, to the point of covering it almost entirely. The mesh ground no longer played more than a very secondary role. This meant also that the motifs were much heavier than the réseau, which was by comparison extremely light. The laces of this period are therefore much more fragile than those of the preceding century.

### Argentan

Argentan was scarcely made except for large show-pieces – such as the flounce called 'of Marie-Antoinette' for example – which were presented by the important manufacturers at International Exhibitions. When it was produced, it used a ground of meshes covered with buttonhole stitches, exactly as in the eighteenth century; or alternatively, a meshwork of double threads developed apparently by the Compagnie des Indes. Most of the Argentan, or point de France as it was once more named, was a copy or adaptation of seventeenth- and eighteenth-century designs.

### Venice/Burano

The celebrated lace school at Burano, an island in the Lagoon of Venice,

opened in 1873, started as an initiative of the Countess Andriana Marcello who wanted in this way to provide work for the fishermen's wives. All sorts of needle laces were made there, at first numerous copies of eighteenth-century Alençon, then later seventeenth-century Venetian gros point. The school also developed its own style, more or less derived from what is believed to have been the old Burano point of the eighteenth century. It consisted of working large flowers, in point de Venise with light relief, on a ground of looped meshes.

Belgian and French manufacturers also produced copies of Venetian gros point, the technical characteristics of which were exactly the same as those of their models from the time of Louis XIV, except that they were sometimes made of cotton thread. In France these laces were called 'point Colbert'.

### Point de gaze

The technical characteristics of point de gaze are fairly similar to those of Alençon: a ground of looped meshes (lighter than those of Alençon); a very thin cordonnet outlining the motifs; varied fillings. The working of point de gaze, however, was carried out with a rich versatility far removed from Alençon's rather dry precision. Further, the thread is grey-white, rather than slightly golden. It was made in very large pieces with designs similar to those of bobbin appliqué, which sometimes incorporated motifs of point de gaze. Much point de gaze was used for the leaves of wedding fans, and fans for balls, since it harmonized perfectly with their sticks of ivory or mother of pearl.

## BOBBIN LACES

### Brussels appliqué, called 'application d'Angleterre'

When machine net made its appearance on the continent at the beginning of the nineteenth century, Brussels adopted it very quickly, and so successfully that the droschel ground which had formerly characterized its laces was rarely made after 1830. By applying bobbin-made motifs to machine net it was possible to produce pieces of large dimensions much more rapidly than before. Appliqué so simplified the work of lacemaking – although properly speaking what was made was not a lace, since it was constructed on a permanent support – that everybody began to make it. The attribution of an appliqué to a precise centre of production is therefore very difficult. In general, however, exceptional quality and a very rich design are distinctive signs of Brussels manufacture.

Towards the end of the century, machine lace imitations could be mistaken for bobbin laces, particularly those of Brussels. Motifs were therefore made by machine and applied by hand to machine net, which was most often left complete on the reverse side, instead of being carefully cut away as it had been several decades before. This latter feature, though not entirely consistent, helps to distinguish these laces from the older appliqués.

### Duchesse

Bruges specialized rather late, towards the middle of the nineteenth century, in the type of lace called 'Duchesse'. It

Handkerchief edged with lace. Needle. 'Burano'. Italy, Burano Lace School, *c.* 1900
Linen or cotton 29 × 29 cm
Italy, private collection

Although the design of this handkerchief could be inspired by lace-designs of the beginning of the eighteenth century – there are the same decorative stitches in diamond shapes, stripes, and minute point d'esprits – the whole is nevertheless typical of a certain style instantly recognizable as that of the school of Burano

was a bobbin lace of the non-continuous-thread technique worked in the same way as Brussels, namely with three-dimensional effects produced by bundles of threads. Its motifs of veined leaves, always the same, contained nearly as much halfstitch as clothstitch. Its ground of plaits, braided in the manner of seventeenth-century laces, gave it a highly distinctive appearance. Medallions of flowers worked with the needle in point de gaze were often incorporated: it was then called 'Brussels Duchesse'.

Duchesse of more or less good quality was made almost everywhere, but especially at Mirecourt in France. Most was made of cotton thread.

Machines could imitate the motifs and meshes of most bobbin laces, but the reproduction of plaited brides was more difficult, and it was doubtless for this reason that no machine Duchesse was truly capable of competing with the real.

## Mechlin

In the nineteenth century Mechlin was made throughout Belgium and elsewhere, especially in Spain and Italy. Its technical characteristics remained the same as in the previous century. In spite of the monotony of its designs – the straight rows of daisies or carnations – it was extremely popular right through the first half of the century. A large quantity was used for trimming peasant head-dresses, and pedlars carried it to the most remote villages. Its availability, and the fact that it was inexpensive to buy, explains why Mechlin lace, although so abundant in regional costumes, was not made on the spot by the peasant-women themselves. Machine Mechlin was perfected as early as 1850–60, and quickly replaced the Mechlin made by hand. In the second half of the century, the head-dresses and other lace accessories of Normandy and Brittany were made almost exclusively of machine lace.

The few hand-made Mechlin laces made in the following years are often attributed in error to the eighteenth century because of the style of their design, inspired by the Louis XV and Louis XVI eras.

## Binche

The town of Binche hardly produced any laces in the nineteenth century. Surprisingly, the machines succeeded in imitating its characteristic 'snowballs' in a very convincing manner. However Brussels lacemakers took up its manufacture again, under the name 'point de fée', at the end of the nineteenth century.

## Lille

The Lille of the nineteenth century, like Mechlin, was an inexpensive lace, with summary and repetitive designs. Its essential characteristics had not changed, but it was now worked only in cotton thread. All Europe made it. Belgium produced it in large quantities, and one variety was destined for Holland, where it was used to trim the great bird-wing head-dresses worn in certain provinces of the Low Countries. This type was made at Beveren-Waas, a little town in the province of Antwerp. Its designs were extremely characteristic, derived partly from 'potten kant' (pot lace), and partly from cashmere patterns that were in fashion in the 1830s.

## Le Puy/Cluny

The Le Puy laces in their most celebrated variety, Cluny, are continuous-thread laces of geometric design – rosettes, stars, ogives, arcs, etc. – containing a large number of elongated point d'esprits (leaves or wheat-ears). The black guipures of thick silk made in Le Puy and its environs appeared to be of the same inspiration, known as 'gothic', as the white-thread Cluny. Special machines with bobbins that travelled in a circle imitated laces of Cluny type, from the end of the nineteenth century, in a manner so perfect that it is difficult to distinguish them from the hand-made form. In spite of this, Cluny is currently the most widespread hand-made lace in the world: it is produced from Finland to Spain and from Brazil to Madagascar, but chiefly as a domestic pastime.

## Chantilly

Chantilly is a continuous-thread bobbin lace, generally in black silk, in which the motifs, worked in halfstitch, are outlined by a thicker thread. The réseau is made of a Lille ground of twisted meshes worked on a diagonal, or more rarely on a point de Paris (kat stitch) ground. Chantilly, like all continuous-thread laces, is worked in fairly narrow strips, which are then sewn together by point de raccroc, worked with a needle in such a way that the join is completely invisible to the naked eye. This point de raccroc, invented in the 1850s, made possible the construction of the deep flounces and immense shawls then in fashion. Chantilly lace was originally from the Ile-de-France, where a traditional manufacture of silk laces had existed

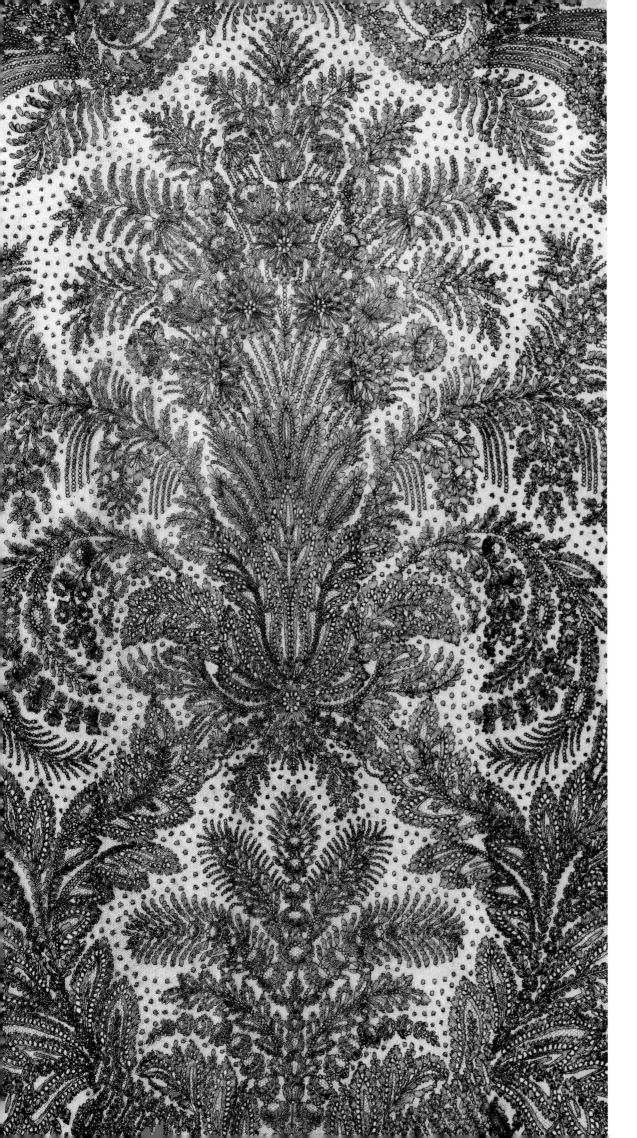

Shawl (detail). Bobbins.
'Chantilly'. France, Bayeux,
*c*. 1860, after a series of
reproductions published by
A. Calavas, Paris, n.d.
Author's collection

This rather unusual design
for a Chantilly shawl is
inspired by the Louis XIV
period, adapted from a
pattern for furnishing-silks
of the end of the
seventeenth century

from the middle of the seventeenth century. Paradoxically, the name Chantilly came into use only after it had ceased to be made in that region. From the 1840s it was chiefly made in Normandy, first at Caen, then a little later at Bayeux, in the Lefébure workshops. The success of Chantilly was such that it was made everywhere, but the production of Grammont in Belgium was the only one which could rival that of Bayeux. It is generally thought that the Belgian Chantilly was more heavily dyed, and consequently a deeper black than the French. The Chantilly of Bayeux on the other hand had a beautiful shade of charcoal-grey with leaden tints.

Machine lace which succeeded in imitating Chantilly in a very satisfactory manner caused the permanent decline of the hand-made lace industry in the 1870s. After that date, only a few prestige pieces were ever made, destined for a very wealthy clientèle or for the showcases of industrial exhibitions. Early imitations were made on Warp Frame machines that produced a knitted effect in the design areas, which distinguish this machine lace from the real.

## Bayeux

The production of bobbin lace at Bayeux goes back to the seventeenth century, but it was not until the nineteenth century, with the setting up of the house of Lefébure in 1829, that it became celebrated throughout France. The Lefébure workshops manufactured all kinds of lace, including Alençon, and one cannot therefore attribute to Bayeux a particular type developed there. The distinguishing mark of Bayeux at this period was the supreme quality of its production, whether this was blonde, Chantilly, point de Paris – a continuous-thread lace with motifs encircled with thicker thread and ground of simple (or double) meshes (kat stitch), like those of Chantilly – or Alençon or Venise.

Page 134
Flounce (detail). Bobbins.
'Valenciennes de Brabant'.
Belgium, Ypres or Ghent,
*c.* 1855
Cotton 17 × 38 cm
Paris, private collection

Lady's cravat. Monogram
BLM, coronet. Bobbins.
'Valenciennes de Brabant'.
Belgium, Ypres or Ghent,
*c.* 1885
Cotton or linen 16 × 106
cm
Florence, Palazzo
Davanzati; inv. Stoffe 2639;
cat. no. 85. Gift of the
Duchess Franca di
Grazzano Visconti di
Modrone

## Valenciennes

The technique of the Valenciennes of the nineteenth century was radically different. It was no longer a continuous-thread lace, but a lace with cut threads (*à fils coupés*). Far more threads were used in the clothwork than in the ground, and the supplementary threads were cut off behind the motifs as these were completed. This method had been invented in the 1830s by a manufacturer of Ypres in Belgium, and it suited the nineteenth-century style of crisply outlined motifs on an almost invisible réseau, as well as being quicker. It also made possible the manufacture of much larger pieces. From that time onward, Belgium became the greatest producer of Valenciennes – indeed, almost the only one, apart from a small-scale manufacture which continued in the north of France. Valenciennes of the new type was known as 'Valenciennes de Brabant' after the province of Belgium in which it was made.

# MACHINE LACE

It was in the first years of the nineteenth century that machine frames were introduced, at first making only net in silk or cotton. They had been invented and perfected at Nottingham in England, and several years later were smuggled into Saint-Pierre-les-Calais in France. Machine net manufacture is based on a system of knitting that began with Stocking Frames of the sixteenth century. At the beginning of the nineteenth, an English workman named Heathcoat had the idea of using bobbins mounted on a carriage in place of the bearded (hooked) needles of the Stocking Frame. The carriage was a metal plate on to which was slotted a thin spool made of two flat circular plates: the bobbin; the weft thread was wound on this just as on the circular spool of a present-day sewing machine. The carriages passed between the warp threads, of which there must be a corresponding number – several hundred or even several thousand – along the length of the machine. This system, patented by Heathcoat in 1809, is related to weaving, but the warp threads, wound at the base of the machine, are displaced laterally, and the weft threads, carried by the threaded carriages on a vertical bar, are displaced forwards and backwards, allowing the threads to intertwine. Numerous improvements were made to this machine during the nineteenth century, but the principle of the carriage and bobbin remained the same.

In 1883, a new technique of prime importance was invented in Germany: chemical lace. The motifs were machine-embroidered in cotton thread on a background of woven silk, then the silk was burnt with caustic acid or chlorine which did not affect the cotton, releasing the motifs from their support. Following improvements to this invention by Swiss manufacturers of the St Gall region, enormous quantities of very close imitations of crochet, Venetian gros point and three-dimensional laces in general were produced.

Around 1830, the adaptation to the net machines of the Jacquard system (of perforated cards carrying the design to be worked in code) allowed the manufacture of a genuine lace – a fabric in which all the elements were executed at the same time, as in a hand-made lace. This technique was perfected from the beginning of the Second Empire, and machine lace never ceased to figure prominently at the industrial exhibitions which followed one another at that time. Bobbin laces in particular were imitated – Chantilly, blonde, Valenciennes, Cluny – in silk, cotton or wool. In certain laces, such as Chantilly, the thicker threads outlining the motifs had to be inserted by hand until the necessary improvements were made to the machine. In France the great manufacturing centres were certainly Calais, but also Lyons, where the big firms such as Dognin and Isaac specialized in articles at the top of the range: the celebrated 'tulle illusion', in silk of an incomparable lightness, was in particular an invention of the firm of Dognin.

Beige afternoon gown bordered with velvet ribbon, with the label 'A Felix Breveté, 15 fbg Saint-Honoré, Paris', *c.* 1884 Florence, Galleria del Costume di Palazzo Pitti; inv. 437; cat. no. 23. Gift of the Association of the Friends of the Costume Gallery

The body of the gown is made of chemical lace, the bustle and sleeves of embroidered net, the cuffs and the hem flounce of machine lace

Flounce (detail). Needle. 'Argentan'. France, Alençon, Argentan or Bayeux, *c.* 1880
Linen
Brussels, Musée Royaux d'Arts et d'Histoire; inv. D.3348

An example of the type of large flounce, based on Louis XVI patterns, that was produced by the best manufacturers of the nineteenth century, especially Lefébure. With the exception of the shaded flowers, the technique of the solid design areas and the meshes of the réseau, covered in buttonhole stitches, is exactly the same as in the eighteenth century. This piece was probably made for an exhibition

Pages 140, 141
Flounce (detail). Bobbins. 'Blonde'. Spain, Barcelona area, 1830–60
Polychrome silk and gold thread 45 × 410 cm
Paris, collection Mmes Carmen Martinez and Viviane Grimminger

The decoration is of cornucopiae, flowering branches of convolvulus, narcissi, roses, pansies and lupins, sprinkled with butterflies, and with a border of leaves and nuts.

The cornucopiae and ears of wheat are worked in gold thread; the ground is in black silk. This lace belonged to the family of the sculptor Julio Gonzalez, a friend of Picasso. Its virtuosity is unique, and no other piece can be compared with it, either for the excellence of its workmanship or for the exceptionally vivid colouring of the design. For a more complete description, see the catalogue of the Lyons exhibition, no. 112

Flounce (detail). Bobbins and needle. 'Brussels appliqué, called application d'Angleterre', on machine net. Brussels, 1855–70
Linen and cotton 34 × 80 cm
Paris, private collection

The flowering branches applied to the net are bobbin-made, while the basket and the knot of ribbon from which it is suspended are in point de gaze

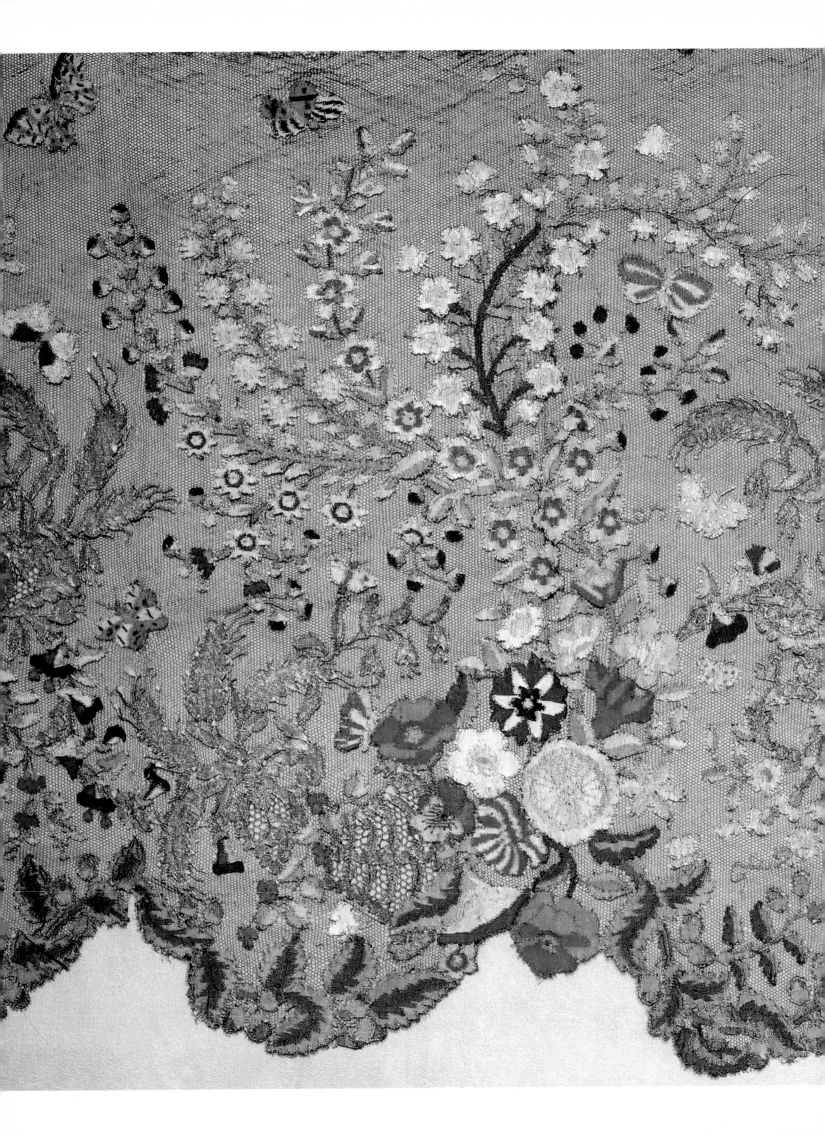

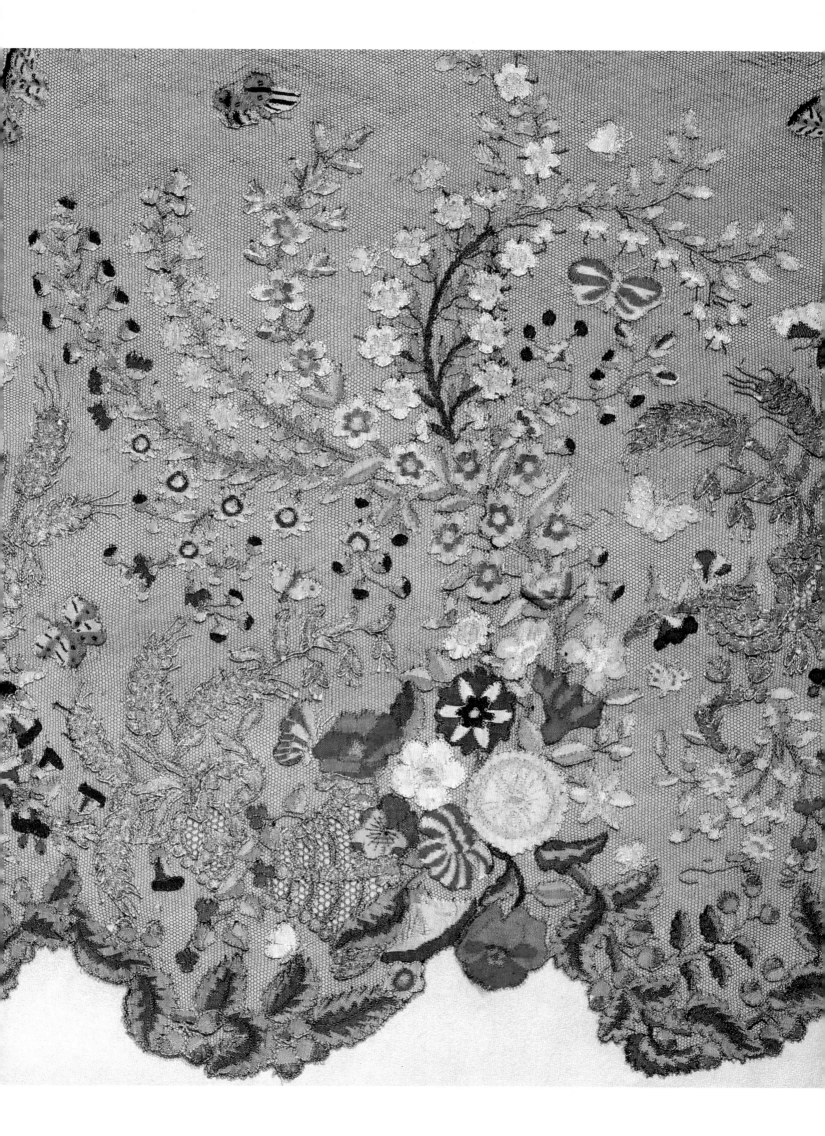

Flounce (detail). 'Brussels appliqué, called application d'Angleterre'. Belgium or France, *c.* 1870–90
Linen and silk 35 × 220 cm
Paris, private collection

The motifs are applied to 'tulle illusion' made of the very fine silk from which it gets its name. This machine net was invented by the firm of Dognin, of Lyons

Flounce (detail). Needle. 'Argentan'. France, manufactured by Verdé-Delisle of Alençon, c. 1855
Linen 67 × 283 cm
Lyons, Musée Historique des Tissus, s.n.

This famous flounce, known as 'of Marie-Antoinette', was made for the 1855 exhibition by the firm of Verdé-Delisle, after the design of a gown or, according to some, a lace, which had belonged to Queen Marie-Antoinette. Later, the flounce was often illustrated as a genuine eighteenth-century piece

Page 144–5
Flounce (detail). Needle. 'Point de gaze'. Brussels, 1860–80
Linen 20 × 480 cm
Florence, Palazzo Davanzati; inv. 3263; gift of Giorgio Calligaris

The design of full-blown roses and ferns is typical of the taste of the Second Empire. Such patterns were produced continually, without modification, up to the 1890s

Shawl (detail). Needle.
'Point de gaze'. Brussels,
*c*. 1865
Linen 140 × 300 cm
Italy, private collection

A bouquet of naturalistic
flowers with spirals and
motifs resembling railway
tracks along the border

Handkerchief. Needle.
'Point de gaze'. Brussels,
*c*. 1860
Linen 34 × 34 cm
Italy, private collection

Shawl (detail). Needle.
'Point de gaze'. Brussels,
1860–80
Linen 120 × 300 cm
Paris, Musée des Arts
Décoratifs; inv. 34376

The rich decoration
illustrates the determination
of the manufacturers of the
time to display the
virtuosity of their workers
to the full, as a means of
justifying the price, indeed
the very existence, of hand-
made laces

# THE
# TWENTIETH
# CENTURY

# ART AND
# FASHION

Letters for incrustation. Needle. 'Point de gaze'. Belgium or Italy, *c.* 1900 Each 11.5 × 40 cm Florence, Palazzo Davanzati

These letters form the word *trine*, Italian for lace

On 26 March 1892, a French magazine, *Le Moniteur de la mode*, pointed out to its readers that 'all our grandmothers' old laces, which have slept for so long in their big perfumed sachets, have a share in the success of our toilettes . . . Brussels, Alençon, Bruges, Valenciennes, the beautiful Italian guipures . . . bring the support of their richness to the simplest of clothes. It's a passion, a rage, everyone wants them, the old laces are on the rise; we quarrel over them, we snatch them. Black, white, russet or greyish-brown, their success is the same.' The problem of the hand-made lace industry is well illustrated in this paragraph. At the turn of the century lace was so fashionable that its hand-manufacture, however intensive, could not supply the quantity desired. As for the demand for quality, that scarcely existed any longer. Machines imitated every kind of lace, even Venetian gros point and other three-dimensional forms. The traditional clientèle for hand-made lace, the aristocracy, now turned to antique laces, with their inimitable style. *Le Moniteur de la mode*, tellingly subtitled *Journal du grand monde*, regaled its readers with details of the reception and wedding outfits of the European courts: Princess Mary of Teck wore a 'veil of old point d'Angleterre' when she married the Prince of Wales in 1893; the Princess of Battenberg was 'in rose leaf Duchess satin, trimmed with Argentan lace formerly worn by Queen Char-

lotte'; while the Princess Christine of Schleswig-Holstein wore an outfit 'in mauve velvet and buttercup satin, with flounces of old Mechlin forming festoons held up by brooches of precious stones'.

Since any ordinary young girl in a gown of machine lace could look like a duchess, the label 'hand-made' was by itself no longer sufficient to justify the difference in price. It became necessary to add to this the value – sometimes economically intangible but always socially real – which attaches to the antique. To give laces that slightly antiquated look which would identify them as family heirlooms, women did not hesitate to steep them in infusions of tea, coffee, onion skins, etc. The resultant russet or grey laces – as they were described in the fashion journal – would have appeared in very bad taste to the stylish people of the seventeenth or eighteenth centuries, who only liked them very white!

It also became the fashion to collect antique laces, and private individuals competed with the big museums to acquire the rarest pieces. One of the first museums in the world to put lace on show was the Musée Cluny in Paris which, from 1851, presented it 'in situ' on a Renaissance bed or table or in display cases. The Victoria and Albert Museum, London, then called the Kensington Museum, several years later organized an exhibition of antique laces, where pride of place was given to the collection of Dupont-

Piece for attachment to a gown. Needle. 'Point de gaze'. Brussels, *c.* 1905
Cotton 6 × 80 cm
Collection Doris May, Boston

This piece in the form of a 'necklace' is intended to be stitched at the top of a bodice

Collar. Needle. 'Flat Venetian lace'. Italy, 1895–1905
Cotton, diameter 35 cm
Collection Jacqueline Daniel

The hunting scene along the inner border is a faithful copy of a design by Cesare Vecellio, published in 1591. The decoration of the scallops is similarly inspired by sixteenth-century patterns: there are Medici vases with S-shaped handles, grotesques and peacocks, as well as geometric rosettes and stylized figures

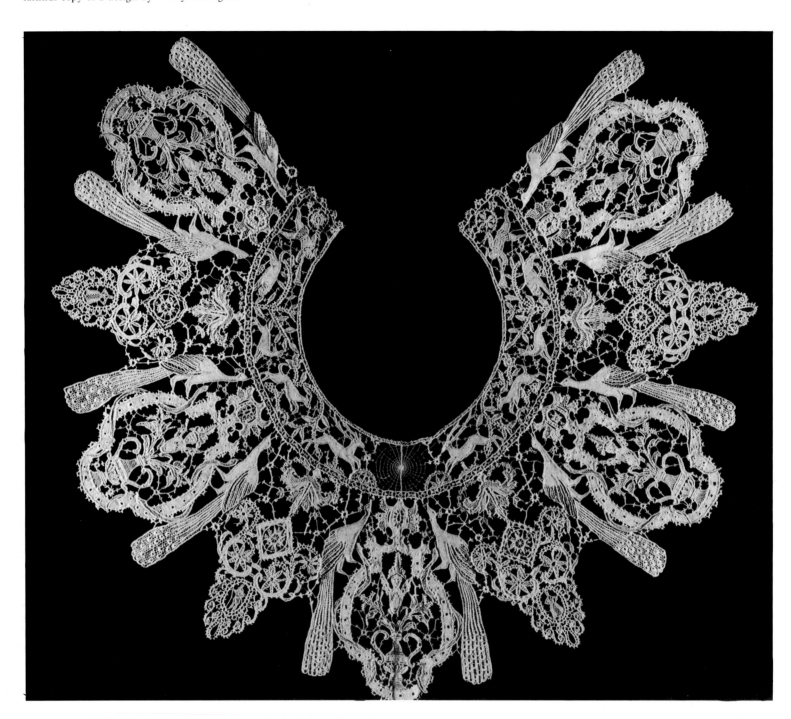

Auberville, consisting largely of sixteenth- and seventeenth-century pieces: this collection later went to the Musée des Arts Décoratifs in Paris. The Musée Historique des Tissus in Lyons bought the Pasco collection from Barcelona; these laces were cut in two, one part being kept at Lyons, the other going to Paris. The collections of old patterns assembled by the great French merchant-manufacturers such as Lefébure or Lescure were given or sold to the Musée des Arts Décoratifs in Paris, of which M. Lefébure was one of the distinguished members. In Switzerland, the firm of Iklé-Jacoby, important manufacturers of machine lace,

Collar. Needle. 'Flat Venetian lace'. France, Auvergne, 1900–10
Linen, diameter 45 cm
Paris, Musée de la Mode et du Costume de la Ville de Paris; inv. 68.72.1

This is probably a product of the La Gergovia school, founded at Issoire in the Auvergne by M. Lescure. The crackly ground appears to have been in fashion from 1892, by which date it was already being imitated by the machines. A crackle finish was also in vogue for the ceramics of the period

formed a collection of antique laces which today constitutes the central nucleus of the Textile Museum at St Gall, and which is one of the most important in the world for the quantity and quality of the examples which it contains. In Germany, the pastor Franz Bock sold his collection of lace, mostly Italian, to several different museums, including that of Düsseldorf. In 1911 the exhibition at the Kunstgewerbe Museum in Leipzig included, in addition to their own pieces, those of private collectors from all parts of Germany. Illustrations of these laces appeared in a series of large volumes with commentary by Marie Schüette, a specialist in lace history, whose publications are now being reprinted. Finally, in America, the Metropolitan Museum of Art in New York assembled some very fine pieces, each purchase or gift being the subject of a commentary in the *Museum Bulletin*.

Between 1890 and the First World War a year never passed without an exhibition of 'Woman's Art' – lace and embroidery – being held in one of the European capitals – and added to these were the industrial or international exhibitions in which the manufacturers, and above all the schools which had now taken over hand-lace production, continued to participate.

Now that antique laces had become museum pieces they excited covetousness. Commenting on the exhibition of 'Antique and Modern Laces' at the Musée des Arts Décoratifs in Paris in 1906, the journal *Art et décoration* warned 'let us be on our guard against fraudulent imitations. Periodically dealers offer collectors or museums beautiful French laces which resemble famous pieces. Where do they come from? Often from Italy, where during the whole of the nineteenth century, the workers, as skilful as in the past, produced a great deal of lace of which

not a single piece appeared to be nineteenth century. Last year customs officials stopped at the frontier a package of 120 kilos of lace declared to be of the seventeenth century . . . showing damage and a patina which had nothing to do with time.' One can only wonder how many laces, dated today as sixteenth or seventeenth century, were not in reality made in the nineteenth.

Only Italy continued to produce hand lace without yet collecting it on a large scale. In 1893 there were lace schools throughout Italy, including those in the women's prisons of Perugia and Messina, where 'antique bobbin laces and Sicilian drawnworks were copied to perfection', according to the Countess Cora di Brazzà, herself the founder of a lace school at Fagagna, north of Venice. They, however, did not sell their laces as other than what they were – modern: the problem is that they are so well made that it is very difficult to distinguish them from the antique.

Burano, the most famous of these schools, founded in 1873 by the Countess Andriana Marcello, was one of the few to develop an immediately recognizable style, perfected

Pillow-case. Needle. 'Reticella' and 'punto in aria'. Bologna, Aemilia Ars workshop, *c*. 1904
Linen 35 × 49 cm
Florence, Palazzo Davanzati; inv. Stoffe 1548

The design of peacocks, vases and iris is from the pattern book of Aurelio Passerotti, first published in Bologna in 1560

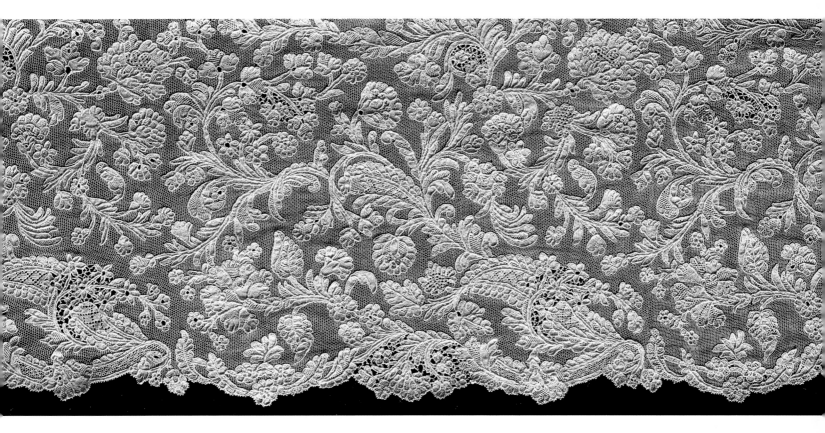

around 1900, while at the same time producing faithful copies of old laces to order. All the Burano laces carried a seal bearing the name of the school on a yellow ribbon. The work of the school also stimulated private production: the celebrated Venetian firm of Jesurum, which still continues, trained workers and produced interesting pieces, notably polychrome laces, several examples of which are preserved at the Musée des Arts Décoratifs in Paris. On the other hand, the workshop/school of the Aemilia Ars Society, founded in Bologna in 1901, made principally laces inspired by or even copied from pattern books of the sixteenth century. All these books had been reprinted in facsimile in nearly every country. The peculiarity of the Aemilia Ars patterns lies in the fact that they interpreted the designs far more literally than was ever attempted at the time. Not an eye was missing from the peacock-feathers flanking Medici vases, from which emerge flowers with precisely spread petals, not a hair was out of place on the

heads of the ladies and gentlemen in Renaissance costume. The technical difficulties which the exact transposition of some of these old patterns presented did not in the least daunt the lacemakers of the Aemilia Ars, who excelled in reproducing figures and animals with complete exactitude where the more uncertain outlines of the period had often deviated. By virtue of their impeccable execution, these laces transcend their lack of originality to become examples of 'lace art'.

For lace had become an art. The term 'art', when applied to it, is both a mark of distinction and a death sentence: a distinction because creative artists found it worthy of interest; a death sentence because although there are fashions in art, fashion does not in any way concern itself with art. For hand-made lace to continue to thrive, it needed markets, and creative laces were from their conception commercially limited, despite the frequent and widespread competitions for new lace designs.

Flounce (detail). Needle. 'Burano'. Italy, School of Burano, c. 1900
Linen and cotton 18 × 160 cm
Italy, private collection

The motifs are copied from Brussels bobbin laces of the late seventeenth century

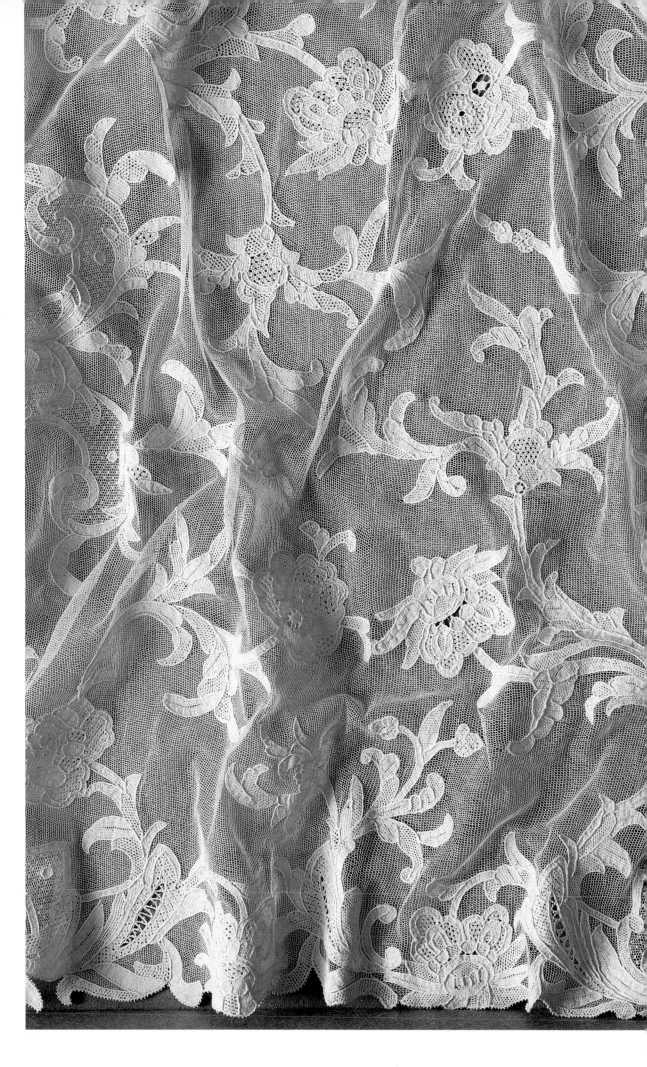

Stole. Needle. 'Burano'.
Italy, School of Burano,
*c.* 1900
Linen and cotton 46 × 225
cm
Italy, private collection

The decoration is inspired
by late seventeenth-century
laces and painted fabrics
from India. The flowers,
treated in decorative
stitches – stripes,
diamonds, 'partridge eyes'
– contrast with the
characteristic cloudiness of
the Burano mesh ground.
Although the Burano
school made all kinds of
lace, this is the most
original, and the most
typical

Lace-merchants were aware of the need to revive the industry, and set themselves to do so. The result of this policy of encouragement of original products was excellent from the aesthetic point of view but less successful commercially. If hand-made laces met with only a limited success, it was primarily because machine laces were able to reproduce the design of any hand-made lace almost as soon as it appeared. It was also because the effort to bring about a revival came too late.

There had been such an excess of lace in fashion that the public was beginning to turn away from it. But perhaps the most significant if least immediately apparent reason, was a social and political one – the trend for women to work outside the home. Lace had long been thought of as a symbol of femininity, but more and more, at the beginning of this century, lacemaking came to be regarded as a supremely virtuous feminine occupation, enabling women to stay at home while earning housekeeping money. And in those times of trade union organization, it could help to prevent women from swelling the ranks of factory workers, among whom social unrest was rife. In France, political figures such as Fernand Engerand, deputy of Calvados, exhorted the authorities to encourage lacemaking in the country rather than in the town, with the admittedly respectable intention of stopping a rural exodus and the breaking up of families. In 1911 André Mabille de Poncheville wrote that 'none among the industries is more fitting to the feminine sex than that of lace. Also none assorts better with family life, household occupations and work in the fields. . . . If one bemoans the introduction of women into manufacture it is not that their material condition there is very bad . . . It is that woman, having become a worker, is no longer a woman.' This argument was not one that women wished to hear. They were asked to recognize 'the great interest [they should have] in extending their hard apprenticeships a little longer, in order to learn to make the more difficult laces, those large and beautiful pieces which the [machines]

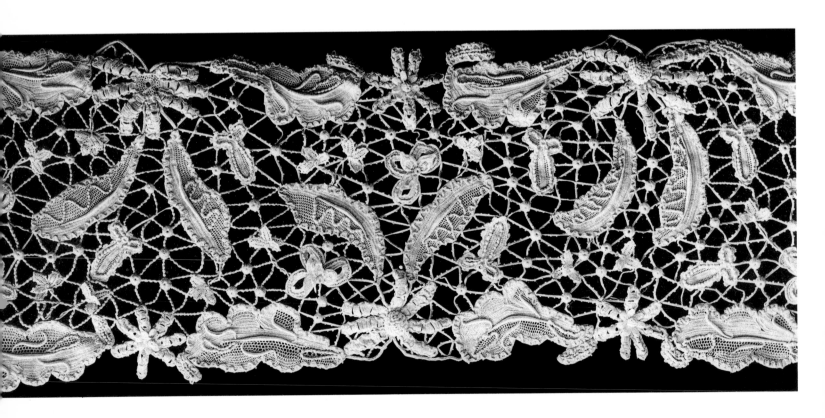

Lace afternoon gown over a cream base. Bobbins and needle. 'Guipure arabe'. France, Mirecourt, 1900–05 Cotton
Paris, Union française des Arts du Costume; inv. 55.58.2

This lace is made of large motifs of bobbin-made tapes linked together using very few bars, and re-embroidered with braids. The little town of Mirecourt in the Vosges made a speciality of these heavy guipures, often used in furnishing. Later Luxeuil, a watering town of the same region, took up this work, using machine tapes joined and embroidered by hand. Such laces, also known as 'Battenberg', are still made today in Luxeuil, and also in China

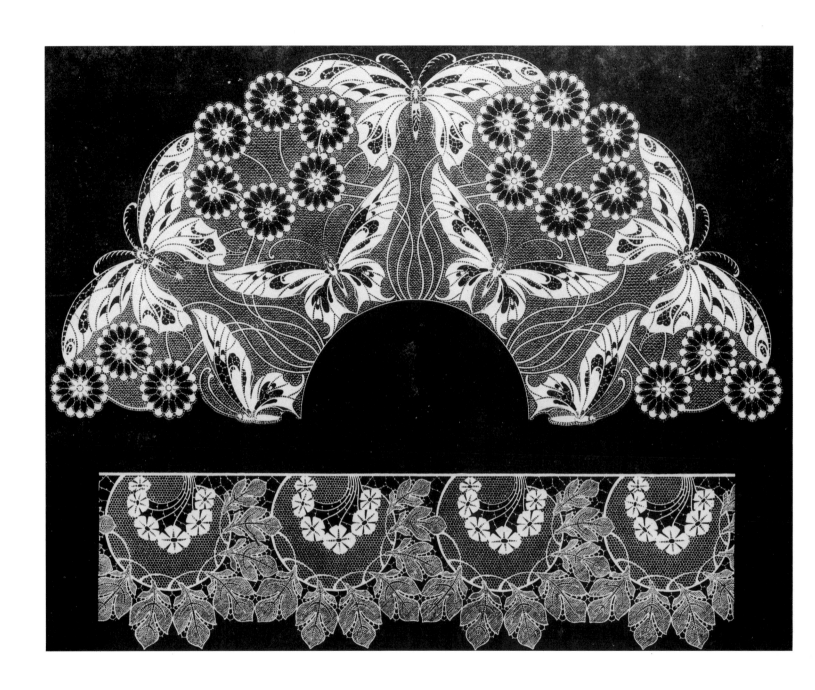

. . . did not even attempt to copy'. M. de Poncheville went on to say that women who did still make lace by hand 'continued to produce small articles of current design' which were worked, 'although by hand, in a mechanical fashion, doomed to imitation by the machine which is inevitably superior [sic]. The cost, for the lacemaker, is misery.' Hand lace of wretched quality no longer nourished those who made it, and not a woman could or would devote several years to creating 'truly artistic' pieces.

Artists now began to interest themselves in lace, and to produce designs in the prevailing Art Nouveau style. France and Austria in particular were prominent in the aesthetic renewal of the art. In Austria, the School of Arts and Crafts in Vienna, the Wiener Werkstätte, included a section for Lace, Embroidery and

Weaving. Directed by a teacher of Czech origin, J. Hrdlicka, with his wife Mathilde, the school produced laces of great freshness of inspiration. The compositions are centred around a botanically precise rendering of plants – umbels, thistles, holly leaves, nettles – with the rhythmic sense characteristic of the Viennese school. Above all, Hrdlika and his two collaborators Mesdames Pleyer and Jamnig understood that the technique had to remain simple and serve the design, not overwhelm it. In 1903 the Parisian journal *Art et décoration* devoted a eulogistic article to the laces of the school. In a famous phrase the author, M. P. Verneuil, described them as 'laces not in a particular style, but which have style, which are not copies nor rearrangements of the old, laces such as indeed have never been seen before . . .'.

In France, the Société de la Dentelle de France, founded after the exhibition of 1904 at the Palais Galliéra, organized competitions for lace-designs. Both the lace schools and individ-ual lacemakers participated. The school of Le Puy, oddly enough, sent a needle-lace tea-cloth in point de Venise, with a decoration of poppy heads, which *Art et décoration* described as 'the masterpiece of its category', though without mentioning the name of the designer. Johannes Chaleyé, designer of the Le Puy school, created bobbin laces of which the best compositions were plainer than those of Vienna, and already heralded the decorative style of the 1920s to be known as Art Deco. The Musée des Arts Décoratifs in Paris preserves a number of these patterns. In 1911 the exhibition of 'Woman's Art' held at the Musée des Arts Décoratifs in Paris included numerous patterns for needle lace made at the lace school La Gergovia, founded by an important merchant, M. Lescure, at Issoire in the Auvergne. These had been designed by a M. Lauret who, if he did not demonstrate a complete independence of reference to the antique, at least was able to apply to them the aesthetic criteria of the present.

Sample of a flounce. Bobbins. 'Le Puy lace'. France, Le Puy, *c.* 1905 Yellow silk and gold Paris, Musée des Arts Décoratifs

Design by Johannes Chaleyé, of stylized roses

At the races. Photographs
taken *c*. 1917–20 at
Longchamp
Paris, private collection

Top left: Dress covered
with black machine
Chantilly
Top right: Ladies of
fashion, wearing antique
laces adapted to the current
style by their dressmakers.
On the left, black Chantilly
of 1870 to 1880; on the
right, Flanders or Milanese
lace of the early eighteenth
century
Below left: A flat bertha
and panel flounces in
machine lace, with large
stylized roses worked in
gold, and hat with
matching lace
Below right: Two lace
gowns with peasant motifs
of Peruvian inspiration

Many of these patterns were reproduced in the revue *Art et décoration*, but unfortunately the originals are now untraceable. Another designer, M. Félix Aubert, supplied very soberly constructed patterns to the Bayeux factory. His fan-leaves and shawls were often polychrome; but coloured lace never really succeeded with the public, if one excepts the woollen laces of Le Puy, made in all colours in the 1850s. As *Art et décoration* explained: 'the pretty pieces where gold, rose and green produce a shimmering effect have only one fault: that of not harmonizing, as do the white laces, with all sorts of outfits'. Lastly, three French designers who concentrated on embroidered filet completely transformed that type of work: they were Paul Mezzara of the famous lace firm Melville-Mezzara, Marcel Méheut and Maurice Dufrêne. However, here again, the compositions were more typical of the style of their time than truly original, and their amusing motifs, rarely used in lace, such as crabs, fish (a skate), foxes, etc., met with little response.

Belgian artists, who were among the most inventive of this period, curiously do not appear to have taken much interest in lace. During the First World War Belgian lacemakers produced souvenir laces with patriotic decorations intended for American soldiers. A German lacemaker, Leni Matthaei, already known before the war for her bobbin laces in Bauhaus style, continued with her essentially linear designs until her death in 1981, at the age of 108.

The jazz age of the 1920s made much more use of lace than one tends to think. In May 1929, *Art, Gout, Beauté* could report that 'one sees lace everywhere, at Nicole Groult, at Dœillet-Doucet . . . Worth has the idea of slipping under the skirts of his tulle gowns a flounce of lace which lightly veils the legs without hiding them completely, and this is infinitely pretty.' Such lace was usually machine made, but it maintained its elegance, since the manufacturers, notably those of Calais in France, Plauen now in East Germany, and St Gall in Switzerland,

succeeded in adapting their designs to the modern style where hand-made laces, with few and rare exceptions, remained traditional in inspiration.

Such hand lace was now sometimes made in areas outside Europe, where it had been introduced by the French and British. Venetian lace was made in Tunisia, Algeria, Madagascar and Vietnam; Cluny and Maltese were made in

Negligée in cream silkskin, trimmed with antique lace, *c.* 1935
Paris, private collection

The top of the bodice is made of a bobbin lace of Brussels Duchesse or Mirecourt type, 1890s

Cloth. Needle. 'Flat
Venetian lace', *c.* 1905
German manufacture
From *Nouveau Choix de
points divers*, ed. A.
Calavas, n.d.

The stylized decoration of
trefoils, tulips, strawberry
flowers and thistles, is
doubtless inspired by
embroidery patterns of the
sixteenth century rather
than by true laces. The
composition also recalls the
designs of 'Liberty' fabrics,
notably those of William
Morris

Félix Aubert. Two gouache
designs: fan leaf or collar,
1903
From *Entwürfe für Spitzen
und Stickereien*, n.d.
Paris, Bibliothèque des Arts
Décoratifs, collection
Maciet

Panel. Needle, embroidered filet. Design by M. Méheut, 1904
From *Art et Décoration*, 1904
Paris, Bibliothèque des Arts Décoratifs, collection Maciet

Decoration of a skate

Flounce. Bobbins. France, Le Puy (?), *c.* 1910
White silk and gold thread
13 × 69 cm
Italy, private collection

Decoration in 'Ballets Russes' style with pointed scallops recalling the shape of the pearl-embroidered caps of the boyars' wives. The Ballets Russes, presented in Paris in 1909, had a great influence on the decorative and applied arts of the period, particularly on the textile and lace industry

India. Brussels was made in China, etc. The lace industry in these countries dated back to the mid-nineteenth century, having been taken there by charitable ladies whose aim was to provide work for impoverished populations. In the twentieth century it was instead a case of an abundant labour-force producing hand-made laces for a wage which few European lacemakers would accept. Some former colonies continued to manufacture lace after independence; others, like the countries of the Maghreb, abandoned it completely. China never ceased to improve its production and to export it. Even today, it supplies most of the European lace-shops.

An interesting latter-day experiment in lace-design was that of Suzanne Pinault in 1933. Apparently influenced by a stay in Algeria and Morocco, Mme Pinault was inspired by the geometric patterns of the ceramic and wood mosaics characteristic of those countries, and with simple techniques – she used only two stitches, clothstitch and halfstitch – composed motifs of stars and rosettes on a ground of twisted meshes which were quite independent of Renaissance designs.

The Second World War finally killed commercial hand-made lace in Europe. In France, the few people who still made lace did so solely for their own use, or for pleasure, with the possible exception of the workshops of Le Puy or Alençon which still supported themselves by selling products to tourists.

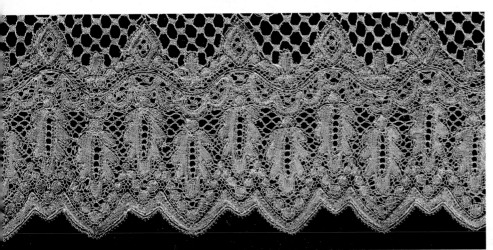

Sample of machine lace. France, Calais, 1910–25
Gold-coloured metal thread
Calais, Musée des Beaux-Arts et de la Dentelle, dépôt légal

The design of this piece is inspired by Japanese cut-paper stencils, used for printing textiles

Insertion. Bobbins. France,
*c.* 1933
Linen 14 × 500 cm
Paris, Musée de la Mode et
du Costume de la Ville de
Paris; inv. 82.152

This lace is the work of
Suzanne Pinault, inspired
by the mosaics of North
Africa

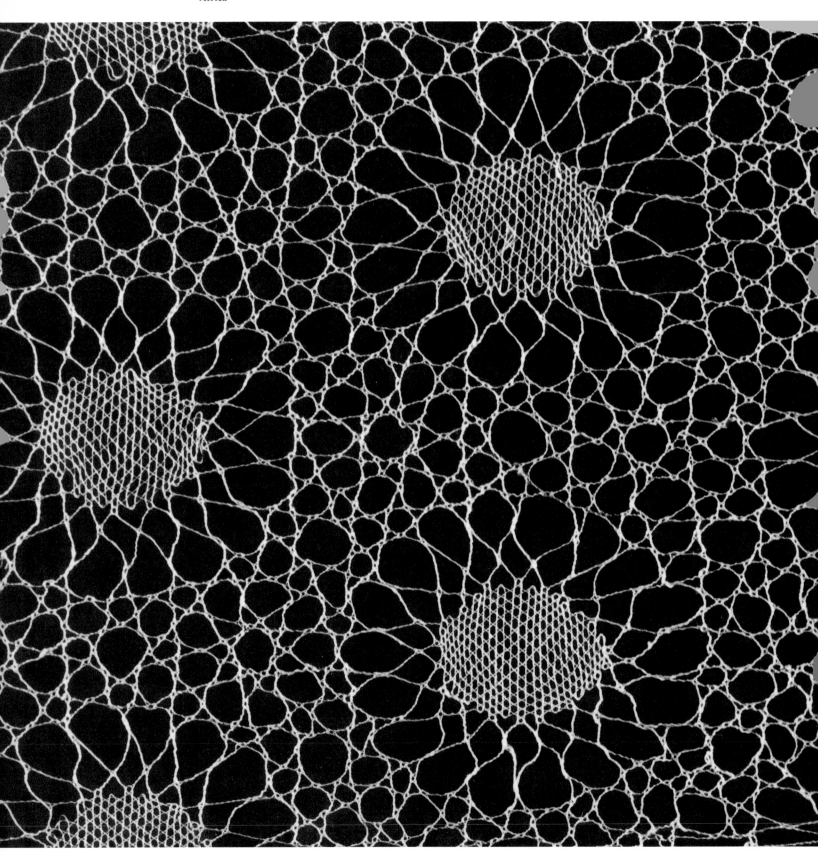

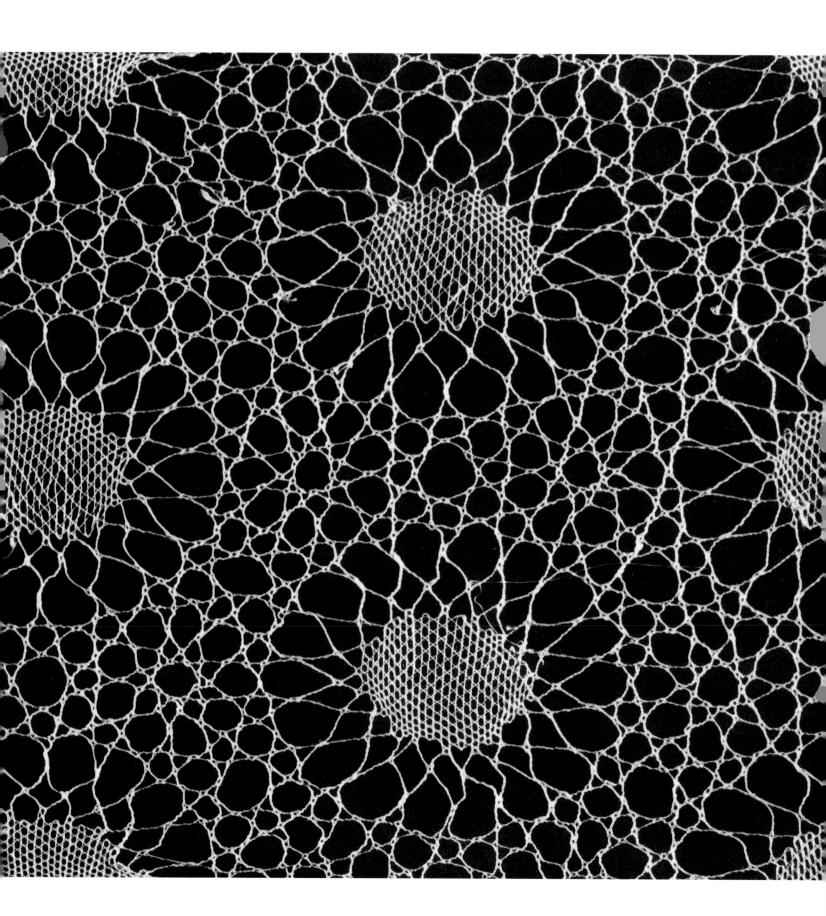

Sample of 'chemical guipure'. Switzerland, St Gall, *c.* 1900
Cotton 19 × 43 cm
North Gower, Ontario, collection Margaret Ruhland

The quality of this imitation – in fact a machine embroidery rather than a lace – of Venetian gros point is such that it is difficult for an untrained eye to distinguish it from the hand-made form. Comparable machine laces are no longer produced

Evening gown in silk and machine guipure of St Gall. Creation by Yves Saint Laurent for Baroness Guy de Rothschild, on the occasion of the Proust Ball, 1971
Property of Baroness Guy de Rothschild

On the other hand, in the 1950s machine lace was doing well. One of the oldest machine-lace firms in France, Dognin of Lyons, founded at the beginning of the nineteenth century, and the firm of Marescot, were two of the most dynamic. Marescot continues today, but Dognin closed, after nearly two centuries, in 1984. The big couturiers used machine lace in profusion on the sumptuous evening gowns that were in fashion after the privations of the war. Chanel adored black lace, while Dior and Balmain loved white; as for Balenciaga, he used all sorts of colours: vivid green, violet, claret, or egg yellow.

Lace had also found an important outlet in feminine underwear, including that fairly recent invention, the brassière. The new technologies developed in the textile industry could equally be applied to lace. The mixing of natural or synthetic fibres with latex, for example, provided another totally new invention, the lace girdle. The couturier Marcel Rochas brought black lace corsets into fashion with the costumes he created for, among others, the actress Mae West, whose ample form was at once restrained and displayed to advantage in this elasticated lingerie. The great stars of the cinema posed in

Lanvin, evening bag.
Machine Chantilly, white
and black, over white silk.
France, *c.* 1950
Paris, Union Française des
Arts du Costume; inv.
79.9.1.C

Suzanne Talbot. Hat with
a veil. Black machine
Chantilly. France, *c.* 1940
Paris, Union Française des
Arts du Costume; inv.
61.12.35

Chanel. Evening gown of
black machine Chantilly,
1957

Creation of Hélène Rose,
1956
Bridal gown of Princess
Grace of Monaco. Ivory
silkskin and lace
Philadelphia Museum of
Art; inv. 56.51. Gift of
H.R.H. Princess Grace of
Monaco

The bodice is made of
bobbin lace of Brussels
Duchesse type from the
1880s. The veil is bordered
with Brussels bobbin
appliqué

black *guêpières* – from Rita Hayworth to Ava Gardner, and Jane Russell to Marilyn Monroe. The eroticism of these photographs was universally felt to be acceptable where to show women posing in white lace lingerie might still be considered difficult. In the advertising of the period the brassières or girdles illustrated were mostly of solid flesh-coloured lace, deliberately shorn of sex appeal.

At the end of the 1960s bras were burned, those made of lace not excepted, and the fashion for mini-skirts was not congenial to lace. By one

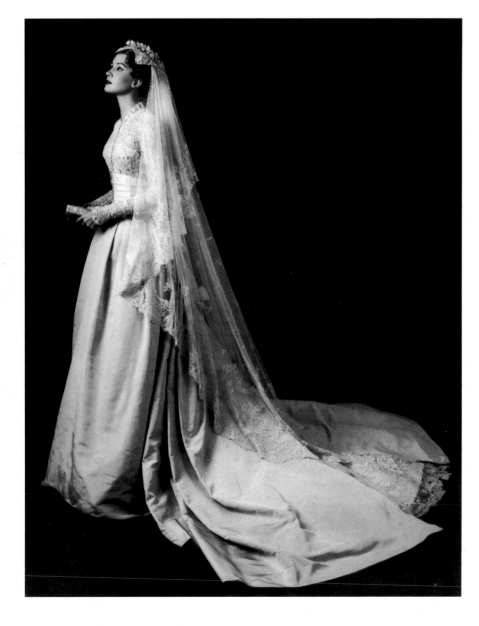

of the revolutions to which fashion is subject, lace in 1970 was somewhat in the same situation as it had been at the end of the eighteenth century: everybody knew what it was, but it was nowhere to be seen. The word 'lace' evoked an image of femininity, certainly, but a somewhat fussy and old-fashioned one. It seemed that even machine lace could never regain more than a marginal place in fashion. However from 1970, when Yves Saint Laurent created his celebrated backless gown featuring black Chantilly, couturiers and fashion designers began to rediscover it, and in 1988 nearly all the collections showed lace. For the first time in a long while, one could find machine laces inspired by Venetian gros points, Flanders laces of the seventeenth century, or rich Brussels laces of the nineteenth century, or even embroideries imitating lace. The come-back of evening gowns and of weddings in white partially explains this return to favour, but it was also used in a totally new manner, with tweed suits and Prince of Wales checks, for example.

All fashions that last more than a season are a response to social phenomena, whether of greater or lesser significance. Lace evidently answers a need for femininity which strongly reasserts itself today, perhaps in reaction to the unisex fashions of the 1970s. But is lace condemned to remain uniquely feminine? For more than two centuries, masculine elegance was inconceivable without it. The lace clothes for men presented recently by the French designer Jean-Paul Gaultier were doubtless not intended to be taken seriously, but in matters of fashion, anything is possible, and the most avant-garde and eccentric styles of today can become tomorrow's norm.

Yves Saint Laurent. Short
cocktail dress in black crepe
and black machine
Chantilly, 1970

This dress was a sensation
at the time because of the
audacious scooping of the
back

Evening gown with a velvet bow by Yves Saint Laurent, spring-summer 1983.
White lace by Hurel

*In contrast to so many rich elements which have lost most of their character as luxuries with industrialization, lace in adapting to the economic and industrial exigencies of our time has retained all its qualities of elegance, lightness and luxuriousness.*

Chanel's observation, written in 1939, applies equally well to the three evening dresses shown, created in the 1980s by leading Paris couturiers of industrially produced lace.

Evening gown, gypsy style, by Thierry Mugler, spring-summer 1984. Red lace embroidered with rainbow-tinted red raffia for the house of Projetys, from a design by Thierry Mugler

Evening gown in Spanish style by Jean-Louis Scherrer, spring-summer 1987. Black Chantilly by Marescot

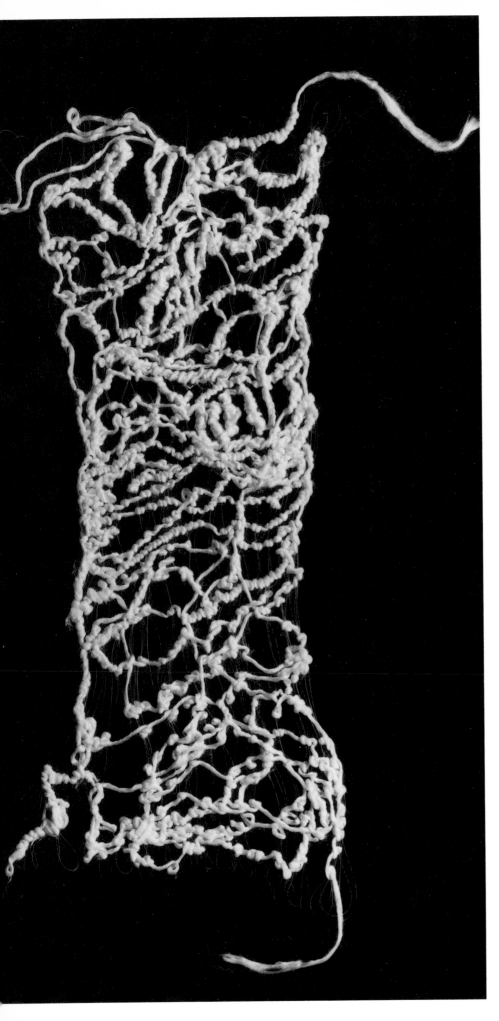

# THE FUTURE

One of the aims of the lace exhibitions organized in recent years has been to provide amateurs and professionals with material for reflection on the creations of the past, and inspiration for the future. Doubtless indirectly rather than directly, their aim has been successful, in so far as artists and designers have turned again to lace. Nevertheless a truly innovative spirit is still lacking, and it may be precisely here that hand-made lace has a role to play.

It is not so much in the copying of old patterns which were themselves for the most part derivative – however fascinating this occupation for those who practise it – that hand-made lace still has a contribution to make, but rather, as in the other applied arts, through the individual creativity which generates a new driving force. Over a considerable period, exhibitions of contemporary work hand-made with bobbins or with a needle have been organized fairly widely, especially in Belgium. The scope of the present work, which is chiefly historical, does not allow description of the pieces exhibited, much less the illustrations to do them justice. However, to show the aesthetic possibilities of the lace effect, if not of lace itself, two pieces have been arbitrarily chosen that embody essential qualities of lace – openness and freedom of movement. Even if lace has not always been obviously an openwork, transparency is the first quality which comes to mind whenever lace is considered. As for freedom of movement, lace is the only technique of fabric-making in which all the threads used are active, as opposed to weaving, where the warp threads could be said to be passive, being fixed at their ends to a loom and moved only as they are slightly raised to allow the weft passage. In needle lace – which can theoretically be produced with a single thread – as in bobbin lace, the threads can move in all directions, including backwards. Even when they are held temporarily in place by pins, the possibility of twisting them in bobbin lace, or looping them in needle-lace, guarantees the independence and solidity

Page 180
Sheila Hicks, *Loose Lace*,
1988
Warp mounted on a
portable frame. 'Weft' of
needle-made buttonhole
stitches. Warp: plastic
monofilament; buttonhole
stitches: silk 22 × 9 cm

This is a miniaturized
representation of a work
designed to have
architectural proportions.
As in a true needle lace, the
support element – here a
plastic monofilament – can
be removed when the work
is finished, leaving an

independent structure.
Buttonhole stitch is the
basic technique of needle
lace

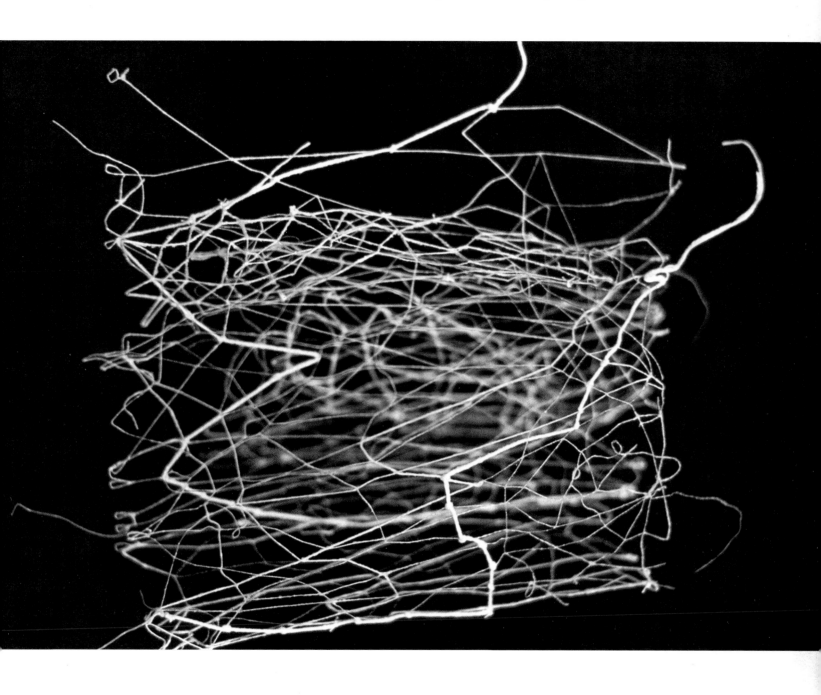

of the piece once the temporary supports are removed.

Every piece which conforms to these criteria of openness and autonomy shares the concept of lace made according to traditional rules or with traditional implements, and such is the case with the two original works presented here. It is not necessary to know how they were made, we need only state that they illustrate these two concepts perfectly. In neither example is the thread-direction detectable, which creates an impression of perpetual movement, while the size of the spaces is an essential element of the structure. The future of machine-made as well as hand-made lace will perhaps depend on experiments such as these.

Marie-Rose Lortet, *Piège-nuée*, 1987
18 × 23 × 18 cm

A three-dimensional work whose evocative title may be roughly translated as 'Gossamer trap'

# Laces of the World

The lace industry in the three great producing countries has already been described. However, it seems desirable to refer briefly to laces in other countries in order to indicate the full social and economic importance of the industry.

## GERMANY AND AUSTRIA

The large number of pattern books published in the big printing centres of Augsburg, Nüremberg, Frankfurt and Strasburg reflect both interest in the technique of lace-making in Germany and the considerable contribution of German designers. However we have very little precise information about the German lace industry. From the end of the sixteenth century it was probably rural rather than urban. We know that the German weavers produced a type of lace woven on looms which must have had some success, since it appears in the inventories of seventeenth-century merchants. Fabrics attributed to Germany are printed with lace motifs taken from the pattern books of Danieli, or imitating Venetian: some eighteenth-century examples are preserved at the Germanisches Nationalmuseum in Nüremberg. In the eighteenth century, the Dresden and Leipzig areas produced white embroideries with very elaborate patterns and techniques which imitated lace. These were soon sufficiently regarded to be copied elsewhere, notably in France in the region of Nancy, and in Belgium. They were usually worked on cotton muslin. In the nineteenth century the lace industry in the Dresden and Leipzig region expanded rapidly. At the International Exhibition in Paris in 1867, lace manufacturers were worried by the formidable competition of these laces, which was due, they claimed, not so much to their quality as to their low price. The opinion of Félix Aubry, reporter of the Jury of the exhibition, was that this competition particularly affected the American and Russian markets. The Saxony lacemakers produced a little of all the commercial laces – Chantilly, Duchesse, Valenciennes, point de gaze and point de Venise. Félix Aubry adds that there were also made in Dresden 'luxury and art laces, reproducing styles of the most beautiful antique laces'. A report published in 1871 indicates that the teaching in all the workshops was carried out by Belgian lacemakers.

Machine lace was introduced at Plauen, a small Saxony town, now in East Germany, in the 1860s. Thanks to a number of technical improvements, the industry developed quickly, and its products, in particular embroidered net, were exported everywhere in great quantities.

At the beginning of the twentieth century, a number of lace schools existed in the principal German towns, notably in Berlin.

As for Austria, we have mentioned the role of the Wiener-Werkstätte in the design of Art Nouveau laces, between 1895 and 1914. After the First World War, another designer, Dagobert Peche, created a number of fabrics and laces, this time with a more linear decoration, intended to be made more rapidly, in embroidered net for example.

## THE BRITISH ISLES

British hand-made laces never offered any serious competition to other European laces. They were made, however, from the sixteenth century in a number of regions, including Scotland, as the stock-lists of the merchant-haberdashers of that period show. The manufacture became more extensive, particularly in the nineteenth century, in the county of Buckinghamshire. A type of Lille was made there, called Bucks point, as well as a bobbin lace called 'Honiton', the name of the town in Devon where it had been developed. This lace to some extent resembled the Belgian Duchesse, the bars and raised work of which were sometimes made with the needle. Queen Victoria's wedding dress and veil were both trimmed with Honiton lace. The designs of Honiton lace are easily recognizable by their slightly awkward style, very different from that of the Duchesse which they imitated; but this lack of sophistication is perhaps what gives the lace its undeniable charm.

In the domain of machine lace, on the other hand, the English were the originators of all the technical developments. Their industry, located around the city of Nottingham, was for a long time more successful than that of Calais or Lyons. The industrial English, more dynamic, technically and commercially, showed an adaptability to the market which the French, by temperament, did not possess. Furthermore, the extensive trade which England had with North America, as well as its immense colonial possessions, provided it with assured outlets, most especially for the relatively cheap products of the machine industry, a situation which was to last until the 1860s. After that date, French, German and Swiss competition became more intense, particularly in the area of design. As with all the other centres of machine manufacture, Nottingham's lace industry collapsed in the 1930s, though without ever disappearing completely; it still exists today.

## SCANDINAVIAN COUNTRIES

Scandinavian production consists essentially of bobbin laces. The varieties most commonly made are Lille with fond clair or fond chant, Mechlin, and the 'pot lace' of Antwerp, as well as Cluny. The designs possess no specific characteristics, being in general derived from French or Belgian patterns. There is however a tendency towards stylization, and towards the introduction of traditional peasant themes. In the seventeenth century, under the reign of Christian IV of Denmark – a particularly brilliant period in Danish history – bobbin and needle laces with vermiculate motifs and an extremely dense aspect were made in the neighbourhood of the town of Tønder.

In Sweden, production was centred around the monastery of Wadstena. These laces differed little from those of Denmark, and equally the types made there were adapted from European patterns. Swedish lace prospered to some extent in the eighteenth century. Laces from the province of Dalecarlia, on the other hand, had a typically provincial character. They are still made today.

In Finland, at present a considerable amount of lace of Cluny and Torchon types is made, and the tradition is doubtless ancient.

## RUSSIA AND HUNGARY

The lace industry in Russia really only dates from the eighteenth century. Before that, most of the laces used in Russia, especially the metal laces, were imported. When the Russian lacemakers set about making lace on a larger scale, they first produced metal laces, then they developed a rather characteristic style of bobbin laces in linen thread, which consisted of large scallops filled with a sort of tape forming close meanders, sometimes interrupted with birds or other stylized animals. Laces in

Bed-hanging (detail).
Needle, embroidered filet.
Russia, late eighteenth or
early nineteenth century.
Linen 36 × 200 cm
Paris, collection Perle Jallot

The decoration, of figures
wearing costumes of the

seventeenth and eighteenth
centuries – a man on
horseback carrying a sort of
racquet, soldiers mounting
guard – flowering trees,
birds and battlements, is
typical of the bed-
trimmings of peasant
homes in western Russia

coloured silks mingled with threads of gold or silver also appear to have been made in Russia, sometimes with a needle and sometimes with bobbins. Russian peasants traditionally ornamented their beds with flounces of embroidered filet, and these certainly date back further than the laces, since their decoration appears to be set around the seventeenth century: the clothes of the people and the architecture of the buildings which appear in the filet are always in the style of that period. The anecdotal aspect of their composition, which seems to be telling a story, the naivety of line and perspective – the birds are larger than the trees in which they are perched, the people stand a head taller than the domes of the churches and the towers of the castles – gives to these productions the fairy-tale air typical of the Slav taste.

As for Hungary, the old Hungarian inventories contain plenty of metal laces, and it is probable that they were made there. In the nineteenth century, Hungary produced laces in the Russian style, often coloured, of which the Musée des Arts Décoratifs in Paris preserves several examples.

## CZECHOSLOVAKIA

In the nineteenth century, the Czech industrial production of lace was concentrated in

Bohemia, in a region then under the economic and cultural domination of neighbouring Germany. They made all kinds of bobbin and needle laces. A report published in Prague (in German) in 1871 took note of the resentment shown by young laceworkers towards the strict discipline imposed in the Bohemian workshops.

But the Czech contribution to hand lace-manufacturer is primarily in the twentieth century. Professor Hrdlicka and his wife, both teaching at the Wiener Werkstätte, were Czech, as was Dagobert Peche, the creator of fabrics and laces from the same workshop in the 1920s. Encouraged by the government, between the wars and after, the Czech lace industry was perhaps the most creative of all. Working nearly always by means of very simple techniques – few decorative stitches – the Czech designers knew how to make a happy blending of traditional motifs with compositions of unequalled freshness of vision (though indeed with a propagandist tendency after the country had passed into the Soviet camp). A little later, in the 1960s, the Czech lacemakers were among the first to tackle the abstract, here also with great success. The lacemakers involved were, among others, Elena Holéczyova, Emilie Palickova, Marie Vankova-Kuchynkovà, Hana Kralova, Luba Krejčí, etc. It is not an exaggeration to say that

these people succeeded in giving modern lace the inspiration which it lacked elsewhere. Unfortunately Czech lace appears at the present time to have slightly lost its creative impetus.

## ASIAN COUNTRIES

Hand lacemaking was introduced into nearly all the countries of Asia towards the middle of the nineteenth century, mostly by missionaries. In China, the industry expanded greatly towards the end of the century, all its production being exported. At first of mediocre quality, Chinese bobbin or needle lace could soon bear technical comparison with the best hand-made lace still being produced in Europe. Aesthetically, on the other hand, they never totally succeeded in finding their own style; their decorations were always adaptations or copies of European patterns – a situation inevitable in craft productions artificially implanted in countries where the tradition did not exist. Since the 1920s, China has provided the greater part of the laces sold in Europe. She produces above all Bruges, Venise and embroidered filet.

In Japan there appears to have been only one school of lace, that of Yokohama, established in the 1870s by the Japanese government.

In the Philippines, where for a long time an embroidery industry of Spanish style existed for the export market, towards the end of the nineteenth century and up to the 1930s, laceworkers produced a kind of patchwork of lace and machine embroideries, making bedcovers, curtains, table-cloths and serviettes. Many examples of these pieces survive.

In India, the English introduced hand-made bobbin lace of Cluny, Maltese, Torchon and Lille types in the middle of the nineteenth century. Their manufacture was carried on in South India and in the island of Ceylon (Sri Lanka). The tradition continues today in the region of Nagpur, near Bombay, and in Sri Lanka.

## COUNTRIES OF CENTRAL AND SOUTH AMERICA

Hand lacemaking in these countries is without doubt more or less contemporary with the influx of Jesuits and other missionaries after the Conquest, towards the end of the sixteenth

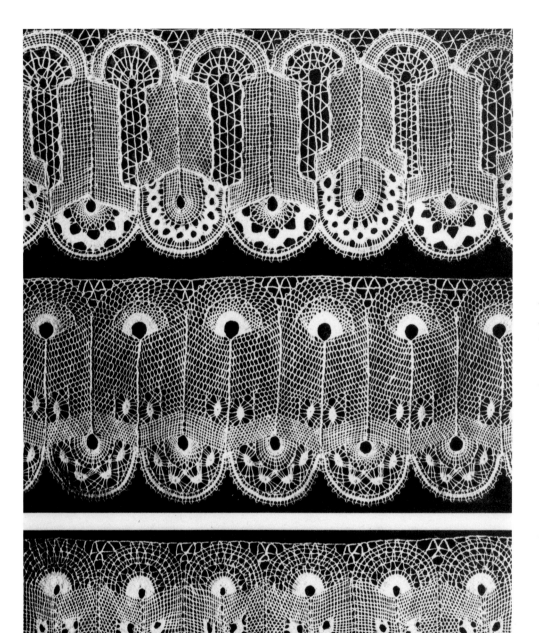

century. However, its manufacture does not seem to have been on a large scale, since the greater part of European exports were destined for these countries. A specific lace, Paraguay – the name of the country where apparently it was developed – succeeded, however, in making a reputation. This was a needle lace worked on a round frame with motifs radiating from a central nucleus. Spain also produced it. A light version, made with very fine threads and with motifs in latticework, is still made in the Azores. Today, hand lace is no longer made except in Brazil, where Cluny and Torchon are produced in the region of Bahia.

## SPAIN

The importance of the Spanish production has certainly been underestimated, at least quantitively. Hand lacemaking probably dates back to the sixteenth century, as it did everywhere else in Europe, and was situated principally in Catalonia, to the south of Toledo and in Andalusia. The celebrated points d'Espagne in gold and silver thread, against which all the sumptuary edicts were aimed, were certainly natives of this country (which still possessed at the beginning of the seventeenth century the largest reserves of precious metal in the world), even though by the following century France and Italy in particular would be producing much more. In the eighteenth and nineteenth centuries, the production of blonde in black, white or coloured silks expanded greatly, especially in the region of Barcelona. Spain also made Flanders, Mechlin, Brussels and Venetian laces. The region of Valladolid specialized in the making of gros point. It is difficult to distinguish run-of-the-mill Spanish productions from those of other European countries. It seems, however, that the lacemakers of this country used for preference for their réseaux a very characteristic mesh with a central pinhole; one rarely finds this mesh in other countries.

## IRELAND

Ireland was making principally two sorts of lace at the beginning of the nineteenth century: crochet, and embroidered net or Carrickmacross. Irish crochet is so universally known that there is no need to describe it here. It was

Three flounces. Bobbins.
Czechoslovakia, 1926
Paris, Bibliothèque Forney

This is typical work of one of the best periods of

Czechoslovak production, when using very simple techniques, Czech lacemakers succeeded in renewing the fashion for laces

Page 185
Design for Irish lace,
c. 1900
*From Dentelles d'Irlande* by Alan S. Cole, Paris, n.d.

manufactured on a large scale from the 1850s, after the great famine of 1846. Crochet was worked principally in numerous convents in the south of Ireland. Its success was such that it was imitated everywhere; it was made in France, notably in Brittany where it became, in a slightly modified form, the traditional lace. It was also made later in Asia, in Pakistan and in China. Unfortunately machines produced a very convincing version. As for embroidered net, the manufacture was centred around the town of Limerick. The convent of Youghal, in County Cork, developed a kind of needle lace of characteristic style. Of perfect workmanship, these laces were inspired both by the flat Venetian and point de France laces of the end of the seventeenth century, and by the bobbin laces, Honiton or Duchesse, which were contemporary with them. The resultant hybrid effect possessed a distinctive character.

## GREECE, CYPRUS AND TURKEY

Cyprus and some of the Greek islands were for a long time under the economic and cultural domination of Venice, and the Venetians introduced them to the manufacture of lace, especially needle lace. In the nineteenth century certain Venetian merchants supplied Cyprus with laces of reticella type. The tourist industry of this period contributed to labelling these Greek laces, although their characteristics in no way differed from those of other centres.

## MALTA

Maltese lace is easily recognized, since it nearly always contains motifs of the Maltese cross and a large number of point d'esprit (leaves). It is a continuous-thread bobbin lace worked in cream or black silk. Its manufacture was imported into the island by the British in the 1830s. It achieved sufficient success, in spite of the monotony of its designs, to be copied throughout Europe, and in Asia.

## SWITZERLAND

The lace industry in Switzerland is very old. One of the first lace pattern books, entitled *Nüw Modelbuch, Allerley Gattungen Dantelschnür*, was published in Zurich in 1561. In the seventeenth and eighteenth centuries, the region of Geneva produced gold and silver laces; then, a little later, around Neuchâtel, linen laces of Lille and Mechlin type were made. At the end of the nineteenth century, the embroidered filets of Gruyère acquired a certain renown. It seems that small boys made them while keeping watch over the cows.

It was, however, machine lace which made the reputation of the Swiss. The industry developed in the first years of the nineteenth century around the town of St Gall, in the north-east of Switzerland, perhaps because that region was for a long time an important centre for processing linen and cotton. The St Gall manufacturers made a number of im-

provements to the machines, which were originally intended for machine embroidery rather than lace, in contrast to the machines of Nottingham or Calais. The Swiss laces in consequence nearly always contained some embroidered areas. They consisted of embroidered net, and laces called chemical, which imitated old Venetian points or Irish crochet, the Swiss machines allowing raised work to be made to perfection. One of the oldest and most important Swiss firms, that of Iklé-Jacoby, devoted itself to establishing a collection of antique laces which today is one of the most beautiful and important in the world. It is preserved at the Textilmuseum in St Gall.

## USA

The only lace centre of any importance in America is that of Ipswich, in Massachusetts. There, in the last years of the eighteenth century, up to 42,000 yards of a continuous-thread silk bobbin lace, of a blonde or Bucks point type, were produced, mostly in black. However the industry collapsed rapidly because it developed just at the time when hand-made lace was no longer in fashion, and was about to be replaced by machine lace. In the 1880s, American philanthropic societies tried to introduce the manufacture of bobbin lace into the Indian reserves, notably in Minnesota and Ohio; but the experiment was not followed up.

# The Making of Lace

## NEEDLE LACE

Lace, as opposed to embroidery, is not worked on a pre-existing fabric, and requires a temporary support which will be removed when the work is finished. This support is the parchment or 'vélin' (today a card is used) on which the lace-design is traced. The parchment is stitched to a piece of strong cloth backed with flannel.

The first operation consists of following the outlines of the motifs by means of a thread, or group of threads (the foundation cord or *fil de trace*), which is fixed to the parchment by couching stitches. To this cord will be attached the loops of buttonhole stitches which form the solid or decorative areas. Each row of loops, arranged more or less closely or openly according to the effect desired, will be attached to the previous row of loops. This procedure can be compared to crochet or knitting, the foundation cord being, in these two techniques, the chain-stitch base on which the stitches are constructed, every row serving in its turn as a support for the following row.

To add relief to the lace, it is enough to take a part of the foundation cord or a row of loops, attach a more or less thick bundle of threads, then to cover this bundle with buttonhole stitches to form the cordonnet (*brode*). The minute motifs in the form of rosettes, stars or partridge eyes are called fillings (*modes* or *jours*).

To remove the parchment once the lace is finished, all that is needed is to cut the threads of the couching stitches holding the foundation cord to the parchment.

Needle lace is worked with one thread at a time. When it runs out, a new thread is simply anchored by a knot – which can easily be concealed – to one of the existing loops. This technique allows several people to work on the same piece, since the motifs or groups of motifs can be separately made and then assembled by a system of bars or meshes.

Venetian gros point. Detail of the fillings and the cordonnet

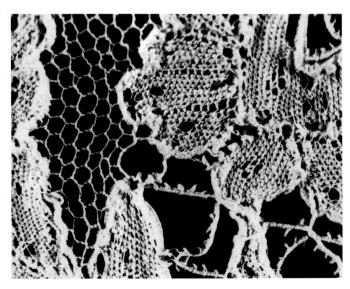

Argentan. Réseau of hexagonal meshes twisted around with thread

## BOBBIN LACE

There are two main types of bobbin lace: continuous-thread (*à fils continus*), and non-continuous-thread (*à pièces rapportées*).

Continuous-thread laces use a constant number of bobbins. This system does not allow the making of very wide laces, for that would necessitate an exorbitant number of bobbins: a lace 12 cm wide already needs up to 1,500 bobbins, depending on the design.

Non-continuous-thread laces on the contrary allow motifs to be worked separately, then to be connected together by a network of meshes, made with the help of other bobbins which are introduced afterwards.

Certain continuous-thread laces, such as Chantilly or blonde, are made in relatively narrow bands, then linked together by means of a special stitch, point de raccroc, which is made with a needle.

The two techniques – continuous-thread and non-continuous-thread – rest on the same principle: the crossing of two or more threads forms a kind of weaving where the warp and weft are built up at the same time. The solid areas of bobbin laces which are called *toilé* resemble a very fine cloth. The openwork parts are formed of bars or meshes, themselves consisting of little twisted strands made with a variable number of threads, according to the type of lace.

The strategic crossing-points of the threads are held in place during construction by pins which are taken out as the work proceeds. The threads are wound on a little spool of elongated form in turned wood, the bobbin, which allows their handling. The bobbins are manipulated in pairs: that is, two in each hand.

Brussels. Droschel réseau plaited four times on two sides (reverse side)

Binche. Clothstitch and spiders

Mechlin. Mechlin réseau, plaited three times on two sides

Valenciennes with round ground

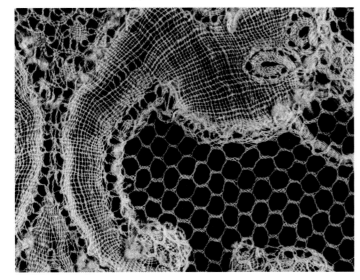

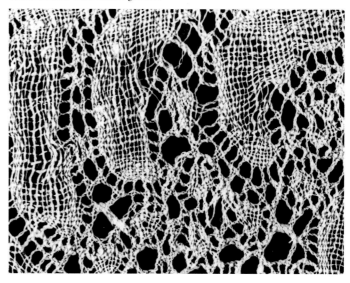

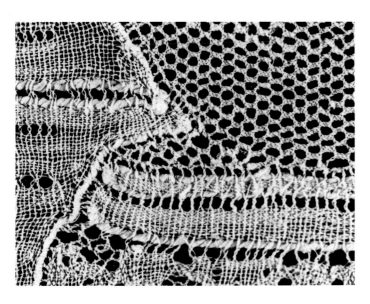

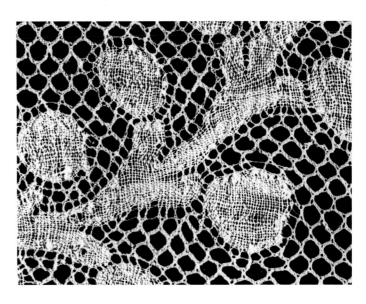

# Photographic Acknowledgments

Abegg-Stiftung, Bern: 89
ACL, Brussels: 138
David Arky: 180
Bibliothèque Nationale, Paris: 15, 16, 46, 54, 110, 113
Bridgeman-Giraudon: 21
Bulloz: 76, 111, 112
Philippe Caetano: 51, 55, 70, 75, 78, 87, 94, 101, 118, 134, 139, 140–141, 142, 145, 149, 165, 172, 183
Henri Cazin: 122
Henry Clarke, ADAGP: 175
C.R.D.P., Clermont-Ferrand: 80
Patrick Delance: 161
Bibliothèque Forney, Paris: 162, 167, 184
Chantal Fribourg: 154, 155, 170
Claude Germain: 37
Giraudon: 18, 19, 39, 47, 50
Marianne Haas: 173
Béatrice Hatala: 24, 28, 29, 36, 121, 128, 168
Kyoto Costume Institute: 80
Lauros-Giraudon: 11, 17, 20, 32, 123
Massimo Listri: 2, 10, 14, 20, 22, 30, 31, 32, 44, 52, 53, 56, 58, 67, 72, 73, 77, 83, 91, 97, 104, 109, 124, 125, 126, 129, 131, 135, 137, 144–145, 146, 147, 152, 156, 157, 158, 168
Marie-Rose Lortet: 181
Doris May: 153
*Museums:*
Musées Nationaux: 8, 23, 38, 45, 62, 71, 79, 114, 115, 117, 119

Amsterdam, Rijksmuseum-Stichting: 25, 103
Berlin (West), Kunstgewerbemuseum, Staatliche Museen Preussischer Kulturbesitz, Psille: 58
Calais, Musée des Beaux-Arts et de la Dentelle: 92, 95
Hartford (Connecticut), Wadsworth Atheneum: 116
London, Royal Collection: 81
Los Angeles, Los Angeles County Museum of Art: 61
London, Victoria and Albert Museum: 68
Lyons, Musée Historique des Tissus: 38, 59, 93, 108, 124, 143
New York, Metropolitan Museum of Art: 82
Paris, Musée des Arts Décoratifs: 163
Philadelphia, Philadelphia Museum of Art: 176
Saint-Gall, Textilmuseum: 27
Claus Ohm: 178
Studio photo Page: 127
Henriette Pommier: 186, 187
David Seidner: 150
Jean-Loup Sieff: 177
Spink & Sons: 60, 65
Patrice Stable: 179 (right)
Laurent Sully-Jaulmes: 13, 33, 43, 49, 66, 84, 85, 96, 105
Claude Theriez: 169
Van Loon Foundation, Amsterdam: 40
All rights reserved: 26, 34, 42, 86, 124, 164, 179

# Short Glossary of Lace Terms

BAR/BRIDE Thread cast between motifs and covered with close buttonhole stitches in needle laces, or plaited in bobbin laces.

CLOTHSTITCH/TOILÉ The solid areas of bobbin laces worked in a manner which gives the impression of a more or less even weave.

CORDONNET/BRODE A core of threads covered with close buttonhole stitches, forming the reliefs of a needle lace.

DROSCHEL Bobbin-lace ground of hexagonal meshes most often found in Brussels lace, the two vertical sides of each mesh being made of four threads plaited four times.

ENGRELURE A very narrow lace, generally made with bobbins, which is sewn to the upper border (footing) of laces, providing a stronger edging for attachment to the clothes.

ENTOILAGE A small bobbin lace sewn to needle or bobbin laces before the engrelure (q.v.) is added. It has almost no design, and serves to increase the depth of laces inexpensively.

FILLINGS The ornamental motifs, as opposed to the motifs of the design properly speaking, in all hand-made laces.

FOND DE NEIGE/NEIGE Decorative bobbin ground formed of rounded spots of various sizes. (Not to be confused with point de neige, a term designating a style of needle lace.) See also SPIDER.

FRAMEWORK/BÂTI Grid of threads made with the needle, or braid made with bobbins, or plait made by hand, serving as a support for the threads which form the geometric motifs of punto in aria.

GROUND/FOND/RÉSEAU Generic term for the bars/brides (q.v.), or network/meshes linking the motifs in needle laces or bobbin laces, worked in various ways according to the lace.

GUIPURE Term derived from the English word 'gimp', meaning braid, applied in the seventeenth century to all kinds of raised laces, especially Venetian, and later to any lace in which motifs are connected by bars/brides (q.v.) instead of by network/meshes.

HALFSTITCH/GRILLÉ A stitch used instead of clothstitch (q.v.) in the motifs of certain laces, notably Chantilly, giving the effect of an open weave.

MARLI A net or tulle with large meshes, woven on the loom from the second half of the eighteenth century, which ended by replacing the entoilage (q.v.).

MESH/MAILLE The round, square or hexagonal unit of the ground, obtained by the looping, crossing, or plaiting of two or more threads, either with a needle or with bobbins.

MODES Fillings (q.v.) of needle laces.

PICOTS A series of simple loops finishing the border or motifs of needle or bobbin laces. From the nineteenth century, picots were often machine-made in bobbin laces. The term is also used of small straight or curved projections covered in buttonhole stitches ornamenting the bars/brides (q.v.) or meshes of needle laces.

POINT D'ESPRIT/LEAVES/WHEAT-EARS Decorative needle or bobbin stitches resembling grains of wheat.

RÉSEAU/NETWORK/MESH GROUND. See GROUND.

SOLID DESIGN AREAS/MATS The opaque parts of needle laces worked according to the Venetian technique, with more or less close stitches; in bobbin laces, worked in clothstitch or halfstitch (q.v.).

SPIDER/ARAIGNÉE/SNOWBALLS Decorative bobbin ground worked in the form of spots, as found in fond de neige (q.v.).

# Select Bibliography

*The bibliography of lace is extremely extensive. Only essential reference works, or those consulted in the preparation of this volume, are listed below. For a more complete bibliography (up to 1906), see E. van Overloop. Catalogue des Ouvrages se rapportant à l'Industrie de la Dentelle, Brussels 1906.*

ABEGG, Margaret, *A propos Patterns for Embroidery. Lace and Woven Textiles*, Bern 1978.

ARSAC, Jean, *La Dentelle du Puy*, 1978.

AUBRY, Félix, 'Dentelles. Blondes. Tulles et broderies' in *Travaux de la Commission française . . . de l'Exposition universelle de 1851*, Paris 1854.

BAYARD, Émile, *L'Art de reconnaître les dentelles. Guipures, etc.*, Paris 1914.

BOISLISLE, A.-M. de, and BROTONNE, P. de, *Correspondance des contrôleurs généraux des Finances avec les intendants des Provinces*, 3 vols., Paris 1897.

BONDOIS, Paul-M., 'Colbert et l'industrie de la dentelle, le "Point de France" à Reims et à Sedan' in *Revue d'histoire économique et sociale*, Year 13, 1925.

BUFFÉVENT, Béatrix de, *L'Industrie rurale de la dentelle dans les campagnes au nord de Paris au XVIIᵉ siècle*. Thesis, Paris 1974.

BURY-PALLISER, Fanny, *Histoire de la dentelle*, trans. the Countess of Clermont-Tonnerre, Paris 1892.

CARLIER DE LANTSHEERE, Antoine, *Trésor de l'art dentellier. Répertoire des dentelles à la main de tous les pays depuis les origines jusqu'à nos jours*, Brussels 1922.

CARMIGNANI, Marina, Catalogue of the exhibition *Merletti a Palazzo Davanzati. Manifatture europee dal XVI al XX secolo*, Florence, Palazzo Davanzati, 1981.

—, *Eleganza e Civetterie: merletti e ricami a Palazzo Davanzati*, exhibition catalogue, Florence, 1988.

CHURCHILL BATH, Virginia, *Lace*, Chicago 1974.

DAVANZO POLI, Doretta, ed., *Cinque Secoli di merletti Europei: I capolavori*, exhibition catalogue, Burano, 1984.

DEPPING, G.-B., *Collection de documents inédits sur l'histoire de France. Correspondance administrative sous le règne de Louis XIV*. Vol. III, Paris 1857.

DESPIERRE, Madeleine G., *Histoire du point d'Alençon*, Paris 1886.

EARNSHAW, Pat, *A Dictionary of Lace*, Aylesbury 1982.

FERGUSON, S. et fils, *Histoire du tulle et des dentelles mécaniques en Angleterre et en France*, 1862.

GÄCHTER-WEBER, Marianne, 'Von der Draperie zum Vorhang', in *Stoffe und Raüme*, exhibition catalogue, Langenthal, 1986.

GRÄFIN PREYSING, Maritheres, *Spitzen*, exhibition catalogue, Museum für Kunst und Gewerbe, Hamburg 1987.

GUIGNET, Philippe, 'The Lace makers of Valenciennes in the 18th Century' in *Textile History*, vol. 10, 1979.

HENNEBERG, Baron von, *The Art and Craft of Old Lace*, New York 1931

HENON, Henri, *L'Industrie des tulles et dentelles mécaniques dans le département du Pas-de-Calais*, Paris, 1900.

KRAATZ, Anne, 'Francia-Italia. 1665–1715: La guerra dei merletti' in the catalogue of the exhibition *Merletti a Palazzo Davanzati*, see Carmignani, *op. cit.*

—, 'Lace at the Court of Louis XIV' in *Antiques*, New York, June 1981.

—, 'The Elegant Art of Lace' in the catalogue of the exhibition *An Elegant Art, Fashion and Fantasy in the 18th Century*, Los Angeles, Los Angeles County Museum of Art, 1983.

—, *Dentelles au Musée historique des tissus de Lyon*, exhibition catalogue, Lyons 1983.

—, 'The Inventory of a Venetian Lace Merchant dated 1671' in *Bulletin de liaison du CIETA*, nos. 55–56, Lyons 1984.

—, *The French Lace Industry (...)* in *French Textiles from the Renaissance to the Second Empire*, Wadsworth Atheneum, Hartford, Connecticut, exhibition catalogue, 1985.

—, 'Dating Renaissance Laces and 19th Century Copies: technical and stylistic aspects' in *Bulletin de liaison du CIETA*, vol. I–II, 1986.

—, 'A French Lit de parade "à la Duchesse", 1690–1715' in *The J. Paul Getty Museum Journal*, vol. 14, 1986.

—, 'An Expensive Affair: The Cost of Elegance in Eighteenth-century France and Italy' in *The Bulletin of the Needle and Bobbin Club*, the Metropolitan Museum of Art, vol. 70, New York 1987.

—, 'The Importance of Lace in Eighteenth Century European Society' in *Dress Study*, Kyoto Costume Institute, Spring 1987.

—, Articles, 'Dentelles' in *Autour du Fil: L'Encyclopédie des Arts Textiles*, Paris, 1988.

—, *Catalogue Raisonné: la collection de dentelles du Musée National de la Renaissance/Château d'Ecouen*: in preparation.

KRAATZ, Anne, and DELPIERRE, Madeleine, *Modes en dentelles*, Musée de la Mode et du Costume de la Ville de Paris, exhibition catalogue, Paris, 1983.

—, *Modes en dentelles*, Musée des Beaux-Arts et de la Dentelle, exhibition catalogue, Calais 1985

LACROIX, Paul, *Recueil curieux de pièces originales et inédites sur le costume*, Paris, n.d.

LAPRADE, Laurence de, *Le Poinct de France et les Centres dentelliers au XVII^e et au XVIII^e siècle*, Paris 1905.

LEFÉBURE, Auguste, *La Collection de dentelles au Musée des tissus de Lyon*, S.I. 1909.

—, *Dentelles et guipures anciennes et modernes, imitations ou copies*, Paris 1914.

LEFÉBURE, Ernest, *Histoire de la dentelle à Bayeux de 1676 à 1900*, Bayeux 1913.

LEVEY, Santina M., *Lace, A History*, Victoria and Albert Museum, London 1983.

LEVI-STRAUSS, Monique, *Cachemires*, Paris 1987.

LEWIS MAY, F., *Hispanic Lace and Lace-making*, New York 1939.

LOTZ, Arthur, *Bibliographie der Modelbücher*, Leipzig 1933.

MABILLE DE PONCHEVILLE, André, *La Dentelle à la main en Flandre*, Valenciennes 1911.

MALOTET, Arthur, *La Dentelle à Valenciennes*, Paris 1927.

MAZE-CENSIER, *Les Fournisseurs de Napoléon et des deux impératrices*, Paris 1893.

MORRIS, Frances, *Antique Laces of the American Collectors*, New York 1926.

MOTTOLA-MOLFINO, Alessandra, and BINAGHI-OLIVARI, Maria-Thérèsa, catalogue of the exhibition *I Pizzi: moda e simbolo*, Milan, Museo Poldi Pezzoli, 1977.

PAULIS, Lucie, *Les Points à l'aiguille belges*, 1948.

—, *Pour connaître la dentelle*, 1947.

PFANNSCHMIDT, Ernst-Erik, *Spitzen, Neue Ausdrucksformen einer alter Technik, Beispiele aus dem 20 Jahrhundert*, Ravensburg 1976.

PIACENTI, Kirsten, ASCHENGREEN, Dr, et al., *La Galleria del Costume di Palazzo Pitti*, exhibition catalogue, Florence 1983.

RICCI, Elisa, *Antiche Trine Italiane*, 2 vols., Bergamo 1911.

—, *Merletti e Ricami dell'Aemilia Ars*, Rome 1929.

RISSELIN-STEENEBRUGEN, Marie, *Trois siècles de dentelles aux Musées royaux d'art et d'histoire*, Brussels 1980. (For a full list of this author's works, refer to the most recent publication. It is unfortunately impossible to give a comprehensive listing here.)

ROY, Hippolyte, *La Vie, la mode et le costume au XVII^e siècle, époque Louis XIII: étude sur la cour de Lorraine*, Paris 1924.

SAVARY DE BRUSLONS, Jacques, *Dictionnaire universel du commerce*, new edn., 5 vol., Paris, 1759–1765.

*Scuola dei Merletti de Burano*, exhibition catalogue, Burano, Consorzio Merletti, 1981.

SCHUETTE, Marie, *Alte Spitzen, Nadel- und Klöppelspitzen*, Brunswick, 1963.

SEGUIN, Jean, *La Dentelle*, Paris 1875.

*The Studio*, Special Number: 'Peasant Art in Italy', London 1913.

VAN OVERLOOP, E., *Matériaux pour servir à l'histoire de la dentelle en Belgique*, Brussels 1900.

VERHAEGEN, Pierre, *La Dentelle belge*, ministère de l'Industrie et du Travail, Brussels 1912.

WARDLE, Patricia, *Victorian Lace*, London 1968.

# Index of Laces Illustrated